01 JUL 2019

- 5 FEB 2020

17/10/22

2/12/22

5/19

This book should be returned/renewed by the latest date shown above. Overdue items incur charges which prevent self-service renewals. Please contact the library.

Wandsworth
24 hour Rene
01159 293388
www.wandsworth.gov.uk

D1362722

GORDON SMITH

Beyond
Reasonable Doubt

A case for life after death
in the modern world, with a foreword
by Maria Ahern, a leading barrister

CORONET

First published in Great Britain in 2018 by Coronet
An Imprint of Hodder & Stoughton
An Hachette UK company

This paperback edition published in 2019

B format ISBN 9781444790924
eBook ISBN 9781444790931

Typeset in Plantin Light by Palimpsest Book Production Ltd, Falkirk, Stirlingshire

Printed and bound in Great Britain by Clays Ltd, Elcograf S.p.A.

Hodder & Stoughton policy is to use papers that
are natural, renewable and recyclable products and made
from wood grown in sustainable forests. The logging and
manufacturing processes are expected to conform to the
environmental regulations of the country of origin.

Hodder & Stoughton Ltd
Carmelite House
50 Victoria Embankment
London EC4Y 0DZ

www.hodder.co.uk

Contents

Foreword

The quest for knowledge has played a major part in human evolution. Whether it be information that helps us understand the mechanics of the universe or something far more mundane, we have an insatiable thirst for knowledge. We are in constant search of the truth and we use different criteria to determine whether something is true or not. In science, we rely on the experts to apply their calculations and equations; we accept their expertise and take their findings to be truth. These findings then serve as proof – until a different expert comes along and gives us a different truth!

In human affairs, including day-to-day life, we approach the matter differently. Though we may rarely give it much thought, we are in constant search of answers, and in almost everything we do, we apply tests to find out what is true and what is false, and these then enable us to make decisions. Sometimes these tests are applied quickly and instinctively; in other situations, the matter requires more analysis. In some areas of life we are conditioned to doubt something unless we see it or experience it for ourselves. 'I saw it with my own eyes' is the barometer test for many of us. But we don't always have the luxury of this type of certainty.

How we decide what is true and what is not has been a subject with which I have long been fascinated. As a child, I was always asking my teachers, 'But how do you *know* that to be true?' Perhaps that is what led me to a career in the law. As a barrister, I am trained to look at the evidence, to analyse it and then to present it to the judge or the jury who will decide on 'the truth'.

In legal terms, we have two ways of determining the truth. In the civil jurisdiction, we determine an issue 'on the balance of probabilities'. This involves deciding whether something is more likely than not to be true and is known as the 'lesser standard of proof'.

In the criminal courts, the stakes are higher in terms of reputation and liberty for some, and in other jurisdictions are literally a matter of life or death. In these situations we apply a much higher test, which has been refined to proving 'beyond reasonable doubt'.

What does this time-honoured phrase mean? Applying the dictionary definition of 'reasonable doubt', it means believing something to be true or correct, even if you retain 'a sensible and appropriate feeling of uncertainty'.

How is this test applied when the stakes are very high? I have concluded that we apply it in exactly the same way as we do in our everyday lives, except that the more monumental the decision, the more careful the assessment needs to be – for example when we are getting married, moving home or changing career. There may be 'doubts', but we weigh them up and consider them according to the evidence and our assessment of it. There may be some feeling of uncertainty, and some would say that this is healthy, since we can never *know* that our decision is correct. But we can use the information available to us: the facts. We can look at the evidence and the source of the evidence. Has a witness a motive to mislead us? Do they seem trustworthy? Is their evidence consistent? Is there corroboration in other evidence that bolsters the likelihood of their veracity? Then we apply the less tangible elements of decision-making: our hope that we are making the correct decision and our trust in the evidence that we have accumulated, having given it all sensible and appropriate consideration.

I have assessed the evidence in this book in much the same way as I would in a trial. There is credible evidence from various unconnected sources that all points the same way, and the evidence has been collated by a credible source: Gordon Smith is widely acknowledged as a gifted medium who has provided many people, over a number of years, with evidence of the existence of life after death.

In my opinion, questions of spiritual existence will remain a matter of some debate for many decades to come, but all we can do, with the information that we have, is apply the same formula as we do in life.

So, look at the evidence, assess it fairly, allow for any sensible and appropriate doubt and reach your verdict.

Maria Ahern

Introduction

Throughout history people have had spiritual experiences and encountered supernatural phenomena. There have always been people who have claimed to see and talk to the spirits of ancestors and loved ones in the hereafter – people who are now known as 'mediums'. Many of our religious books are filled with stories of seers and others who have had visions of disembodied spirits and 'talked to the gods', receiving messages about life and love and hope, and even prophecies of change to help guide humanity away from impending disasters or inappropriate living.

Way back in time, megalithic tombs were places where people went to consult their forefathers. In ancient China, people communicated with their ancestors by carving questions on turtle shells, heating them until they cracked and then interpreting the patterns. In ancient Greece and Rome, people consulted oracles in places like Delphi, hoping for communications from gods and ancestors. In the Bible, at the request of King Saul, the Witch of Endor raised the spirit of the prophet Samuel, and in the Gospel of St Matthew there is an account of the dead walking the streets after the death of Jesus.

There have always been inexplicable rappings, too, and sightings of objects moving by themselves. The second-century Greek geographer Pausanias left a detailed description of what we might today call poltergeist phenomena, and the same sort of disturbances caused uproar in eighteenth-century England in the boyhood home of the Wesley brothers who went on to found Methodism.

To this day, tribal cultures have their shamans, who deliberately induce trances, or dreamlike states of mind, to communicate with ancestors or other spirits with the purpose of gaining their approval or advice on how to steer their people through difficult times and educate them on the rights and wrongs of their lives.

In olden times, such people could be heralded as saints or derided as heretics, depending on the spirits they cavorted with and the messages they dished out. If they claimed they received information from the gods or religious figures of their region, they might be lifted up to sainthood if their predictions came to pass and their messages pleased the people. But if their messages were said to come from the unknown or from a spirit of no high rank, the outcome might be very different, and the messenger might find themselves labelled a necromancer or heretic and in danger of a violent and abrupt end. It's interesting to think that Joan of Arc could be burned as a witch for hearing spirits and then given a sainthood for the same reason. What changed?

In those days, more or less everyone believed in the supernatural, so proving it didn't seem necessary, but by the mid-nineteenth century, faith was falling away and the Church no longer seemed able to provide people with the direct spiritual experiences they craved. There was a spirit of exploration in the air, and science was challenging people to question old beliefs and practices and to think about things in a more rigorous and systematic way.

It was in this context that Spiritualism, with its séances

and spirit rappings, took the world by storm. Séances could include communication with the dead, clairvoyance, prediction, levitation and other manifestations of the supernatural, and unsurprisingly this led to Spiritualism becoming a very popular movement. Leading public figures of the day engaged with it, including Abraham Lincoln, Queen Victoria, William Gladstone and Charles Dickens.

Not only famous figures, but everyday people had outstanding psychic experiences and were witness to supernatural events that made a strong case for the survival of the human spirit after death and indicated that there was far more to the universe than was dreamed of by materialistic science.

It could be argued that there is no real way of knowing how accurate reports of these events were, or in fact if the events ever took place at all. However, as a medium and psychic myself, I have known many of the great mediums of the previous generation, and they in turn knew many of the legendary mediums of earlier times. In this book I wish to reveal some of the great messages that I either know to be true first hand or can say have been passed to me by very good witnesses, either by word of mouth or through the written testimony of books and records kept by people who did not set out to be convinced by mediums, but who nevertheless were.

Furthermore, when the Spiritualist movement began, people were starting to think about the supernatural in a scientific way, and to regulate and measure it, or at least to investigate whether this was possible. These investigations are ongoing to this day. I have been practising as a medium for over thirty years now and have taken part in scientific experiments with Archie Roy, Professor Emeritus of Astronomy at Glasgow University, and undergone a variety of other tests on my abilities, as it is as important for me to understand my gift as it is to prove it to the people I share it with.

In my time as a practising medium I have come across some amazing mediums and other special people who could heal the sick or give accurate prophecies. I have also found many so-called mediums to be charlatans and fraudsters, and I can honestly tell you that it is very easy for me to spot those who set out to hoodwink others for personal gain or reputation.

On my own journey I have been called a heretic, a fraud, a gifted truth-teller and even a saint. For me, there is only one way to prove what I do, and that is to demonstrate my abilities to the people who will truly benefit from them, and those are the bereft.

As a medium, my role is to work as a conduit between two worlds – the world we live in and the spirit world. I have always had the ability to allow spirits to use my mind to give messages to their relatives on Earth, and what I have come to know is that there is a common thread that connects every message I have passed, and that thread is healing the grief of the person who is seeking my help. My most meaningful messages are those that help someone who feels their life has come to a stop because of the loss of a loved one, and set them back on the road of life again. It is not my wish to convert people, but to help them understand that there is more to life than we know.

I myself have been inspired not only by the spirit messages that have come through me, but by the very special mediums I have encountered on my path and have learned about from others. Scientific testing has shown that many of these have had outstanding abilities but, for the most part, supernatural events take place spontaneously and unexpectedly. In everyday life, the criterion we most often use to decide whether or not a claim is true is the test of a court of law. So, as you read on, I would like you to consider the claim that there are genuine spiritual and supernatural events in the world and that spirit communication is possible.

Is this true beyond reasonable doubt?

I

A Time of Awakening

Let me start by saying I don't believe that it is difficult for the higher mind of spirit, or the spirit world, as it is commonly known, to communicate with us; in fact, I believe this has been happening ever since we arrived in this world. I would consider that 'spirit' has been quietly influencing the minds of people we consider to be great – amazing inventors, learned philosophers, brilliant artists and scientists – and moving us forward for as long as we have been here. But in this book I am specifically going to consider the popular movement that became known as Spiritualism.

It exploded into the world in the mid-19th century, at a time of awakening and discovery in many areas. New forms of transport were being developed, new lands were being settled and new ways of thinking were opening up fresh possibilities, both scientifically and philosophically. In so many ways it seemed a time of huge progress. With the gift of hindsight, we can see there was a pattern to all this – the awakening of the mind to new thoughts and phenomena. I tend to think that this expansion of consciousness allowed the spirit world to start to build bridges of communication between their world and ours.

The John the Baptist of Spiritualism

I believe that it is quite clear to see that a momentum of spiritual activity was building in the mid-nineteenth century when we consider the emergence of a whole range of seers and occultists – for example, Andrew Jackson Davis, who is often referred to as the John the Baptist of Spiritualism, the herald who prepared the way.

Born in the Blooming Grove, New York, in 1826, Jackson Davis was a poor scholar and spent little time at school, but as a boy he received guidance from spirit voices. He was said to have a strong clairvoyant ability and the gift of second sight, yet it wasn't until he became attracted to hypnosis, or mesmerism as it was known then, in 1843, that he truly began to display his abilities as a channel while in an altered state of mind. In one of his early trances he was said to have diagnosed people's diseases and prescribed treatments for them, as well as read from a newspaper while blindfolded.

Davis went on to produce a range of trance communications, which, he claimed, were heavily influenced by the Swedish seer Emmanuel Swedenborg. One of the fascinating claims he made after a strange trance episode in 1844 was that he had met and spoken with Swedenborg, who had died in 1772.

Swedenborg was educated in science, theology and other subjects, and this might explain the intellect behind the work that was produced through Davis. There are volumes of writings on both these men, and many accounts of their seership and prophetic abilities by credible witnesses. Both men seem to talk about the beginning of new religions and spiritual progress for humanity. Could there be a thread running from Swedenborg's teachings to the mind of Andrew Jackson Davis?

Some eminent figures of the time, such as Dr George Bush, Professor of Hebrew at New York University, believed Davis's trance communications to be important spiritual works. In 1846 these appeared in book form as *The Principles of Nature*. It received some great reviews and was popular as a new look at spiritual science, but many scientists of the day claimed it was flawed in its analysis of scientific facts and contained psychic gobbledygook.

As a medium myself, I would have to consider, when looking at some of Davis's work, the intelligence and knowledge on display – knowledge that a poorly educated man of the time could not have acquired by normal means. The content of his work did seem to be much more advanced than he could have manufactured, and this has been a pattern that has accompanied many true mediums as time has gone by.

Remember, too, that even the clearest of channels can be distorted in long sessions of trance communication, as a spirit communicator still has to work through a human mind. Also, Davis's book was dictated through episodes of mediumship that took place over more than fifteen months. I would have to assume that there would be errors or distortion in the communication over such a long period. It is very unlikely to remain at a consistent level.

With this in mind, though, I would stress that much of Davis's work is in a style that I honestly do not consider could have come from his own brain, based on the evidence of witnesses who assessed his mental aptitude at the time.

One of the most curious and possibly significant things

that has come down to us from Davis is a section from his diary dated 31 March 1848. On that morning he wrote:

> *About daylight this morning a warm breathing passed over my face and I heard a voice, tender and strong, saying, 'Brother, the good work has begun. Behold, a living demonstration is born.' I was left wondering what could be meant by such a message?*

This was also the day when the Fox sisters in Hydesville, New York, experienced what is now thought of as the first demonstration of spirit communication through rapping. More on this later, but what is interesting to note here is that a year before this experience, Davis proclaimed during one of his trance sessions that the spirit world was preparing a way to communicate directly with people through certain instruments who would be chosen to demonstrate medium-ship for people on this side. So, Andrew Jackson Davis proclaimed the arrival of Spiritualism before it had begun, and on the very day that is thought to be its birth, he unknow-ingly got his confirmation.

As with all of the early mediums and exponents of spiritual and psychic phenomena, Davis's work can only be judged through witness statements, and we have to consider their credibility, but his legacy lives on, as do the many books he compiled through his mediumship. Having read these works and the testimony written about his char-acter, I believe that he was a gifted medium who served the purpose of preparing the minds of those who would listen before the phenomenon of spirit communication flooded the minds of millions.

The Birth of Spiritualism

Modern Spiritualism, as I have already mentioned, was born in America on 31 March 1848 with the Fox family in a small home in Hydesville, New York. They had been disturbed by mysterious rapping noises ever since they had moved into the house, and the previous tenants, a family named Weekman, had encountered the same phenomena. Eventually, the Fox daughters Maggie and Kate, aged fifteen and twelve, asked the 'invisible spirits' to copy the sound they made when they snapped their fingers. The sound was copied, and the girls were able to create a language of raps: one rap when the answer to a question was no, two raps for yes.

Intrigued, their mother asked the spirits to tell her how many children she had. When the answer came back, 'Seven,' she thought it was wrong, then remembered that one of her children had passed away. She asked for the ages of her children to be rapped out, and all the correct answers came back, including the age of the child in spirit.

It wasn't long before neighbouring people were attracted to the new form of communication and keen to try it out for themselves. One of them, William Duesler, had lived in the house himself about seven years previously and not been bothered by any disturbances. Curious about what might have happened there since, he not only researched all the subsequent tenants but also asked questions of the noisy spirit. During this session he was able to piece together that it was the spirit of a pedlar, Charles B. Rosna, who claimed that he had been murdered by a blacksmith, John C. Bell, who had been living in the house five years earlier, and his body had been buried in the cellar.

Later there was an excavation of the cellar and human

remains were uncovered, including part of a skull. The remains were presumed to be those of the spirit who was communicating, but there was controversy over them, with some people claiming they were animal bones. Excavations were carried out on several different occasions, but were inconclusive.

Fifty years later, when the house was deserted and falling into ruin, some children playing there noticed what looked like human remains in a cavity in the walls. The owner, William H. Hyde, investigated and discovered a complete human skeleton minus part of the skull, along with a pedlar's tin pack, of the type that had been used half a century earlier.

The skeleton had been placed behind a wall that had been built after the outer wall, and the assumption was that the pedlar's body had originally been buried in the cellar but had been exhumed at some point and sealed up in a safer place.

Although the pedlar's spirit hadn't given the full story, the fact that human remains were found where the body was said to be buried can be seen as evidence that the information from the disembodied spirit was in fact accurate. An intelligent force was reacting to questions and giving evidence of something that hadn't been known before.

This incident gave birth to a form of mediumship known as 'spirit rapping'. It looks to me as though the spirit world was knocking on the door of human consciousness and the best way to get our attention was to make a lot of noise!

The Fox sisters themselves had so much attention that they went to live with their elder sister, Leah, in Rochester, New York, but the rappings continued, as did the investigations. A Quaker called Isaac Post suggested asking for words and names using raps for letters – one rap for 'A' and so on. This produced a wealth of details from several spirits who appeared to be communicating with the sisters.

Around this time many other people came out of the woodwork and claimed that spirits were trying to communicate with them. Spirit rapping exploded in America and was soon a worldwide phenomenon. The spirits suggested the Fox sisters conduct séances for spirit communication and eventually all three sisters held séances and other gatherings for the public and toured professionally to packed houses.

Maggie eventually married an older man who believed she was a fraud, though he confessed he could not work out how it was done. He encouraged her to give up Spiritualism and she eventually did. Kate, however, continued holding séances and developing her spirit communication skills, including giving messages both verbally and by writing them down, occasionally at the same time.

The movement went from strength to strength. Development groups or circles were set up to help mediums develop their abilities, famous mediums were asked to demonstrate their gifts at high society gatherings, and everyone was talking about it.

Inevitably many people, including the very intelligent, rich and influential, were drawn to finding out more for themselves. To take just one example, Robert Dale Owen, founder of the Co-operative movement, was interested in Spiritualism and produced a pamphlet on it, *Footfalls on the Boundary of Another World*, in 1860.

Some of the finest scientific minds of the day applied themselves to investigating the phenomena. The naturalist Alfred Russel Wallace, who conceived the theory of evolution around the same time as Charles Darwin, was keen to examine it from a scientific perspective. In 1862, the psychic investigation society known as the Ghost Club was set up in London, with Charles Dickens as one of the founding members, and the influential Society for Psychical Research (SPR) was founded twenty years later.

The early psychic investigators were leading thinkers of the time. The SPR brought together scholars, philosophers and scientists, including the Cambridge scholar Frederic Myers, the physicists William Barrett and Lord Rayleigh, and the philosopher Arthur Balfour, who was British prime minister from 1902 to 1905.

The interesting thing for me is that the scientists of the time were not only investigating Spiritualism but also considering ways of creating a machine which could capture and transmit the voices of the spirits they thought were living in the ionised atmosphere around us. Many of the great scientists who worked on the invention of the telegraph and subsequently radio had an interest in investigating mediums for this reason. Men such as Sir Oliver Lodge, who was responsible for creating the components that led to the generation of radio waves, and Marconi himself, were highly involved in psychical research.

There are hundreds of books telling thousands of stories of spirit messages from this era, and some of these messages have great merit while others are clearly fake, but one thing is certain, and that is that people were beginning to look for spiritual answers for themselves, rather than consulting religious authority. This was an undoubted spiritual change.

2

Amazing Phenomena

Spiritualism grew a great deal at the end of the nineteenth and beginning of the twentieth century and it appeared that the spirit world was actually working on the skills of mediums to suit the times and improve communication.

Then as now, mediums came in all shapes and forms, and the act of mediumship also varies, depending on the medium in question. This can seem complicated and in fact I am often asked what is the difference, if any, between mediums, seers and psychics. Briefly, a medium is someone who tunes in to the spirit world and asks to get information about relatives or loved ones on the other side. They act as an intermediary between the worlds – a messenger. They can give you detailed evidence, such as your loved one's name, connection to you, how they lived and how they died. Such information should be strong enough to convince you that the medium is truly connected to the consciousness of your loved one who has passed on. I really feel that if a person is demonstrating any faculty of mediumship, they should be able to give convincing evidence from the spirit who is communicating. If a medium is just saying, 'I have a spirit here who loves you,' that won't cut the mustard.

A psychic won't be passing on information from departed loved ones, but will be able to gain information in a way that is beyond the realm of the physical senses. If you're looking to get answers about your life or your future, then a genuine psychic might be able to help you, as they will be able to tune in to your past, present and maybe even future. But, in the same way that a medium must convince you that they are tuned in to your loved one before passing a message to you from them, a psychic must convince you that they are truly tuned in to your life before passing on information about your future. Then you should be able to have faith in the information they present to you about your future. This is one way you can define a genuine psychic, especially when it comes to readings.

Many people throughout history have predicted future events, from religious men to the gypsy in the street who will offer to tell a person's future for payment. 'Seers' like this won't have undergone the process of psychic development that mediums undertake, refining their abilities in a development circle. Before the founding of the Spiritualist National Union (SNU) in 1901, however, no firm distinctions were made, and those who claimed to be mediums were tarred with the same brush as psychics and seers.

However they were known, at the outset of the Spiritualist movement, mediums produced dense noisy phenomena in their communications with the spirit world. Tables turned, raps rapped and voices were heard. Objects would levitate and hands, or other body parts, would appear out of thin air. Voices would be heard, sometimes using cones, or 'trumpets', as megaphones. All this was known as 'physical mediumship'.

One man who genuinely shocked some of the most eminent men of his day with his ability to produce astounding feats of physical mediumship was Daniel Dunglas Home.

'Impossible to the Rational Mind'

Daniel Dunglas Home, pronounced Hume, was born in Currie near Edinburgh on 20 March 1833. He came from a large family and was fostered out to an uncle and aunt, who moved to Connecticut in the United States. By the time he was a teenager, so much spiritual activity was going on around him that his aunt asked him to leave home.

It seemed that his very presence caused phenomena to occur. He soon became a sought-after medium, and eventually the guest of many royal households throughout Europe. Unlike so many others of his day, he didn't demand that the lights be turned low, instead preferring to perform his amazing feats in the light; he never charged directly for his services; he held his séances at his sitters' homes rather than his own; and he always allowed his skills to be tested under scientific conditions.

In his deeper trances, spirits used his voice to speak directly to their loved ones, and complete conversations would take place between them. When his trance state was lighter and he was more conscious, objects, including heavy items of furniture, might levitate in rooms where he was sitting. He himself would often be seen to leave the ground and float around a room in front of many witnesses. At one séance in 1868 he is said to have floated out of a third-storey window and floated back in through another one. During his séances, objects in the room, when not levitating of their own accord, would appear to be stuck to the table and would defy gravity when the table would raise itself to a vertical position. Musical instruments would play independently of people and spirit voices would be heard, again without assistance of the medium.

From my studies of mediums and their abilities, I feel in my heart that this man was something more than just a medium. I obviously haven't witnessed his gifts first hand, or talked to anyone who has, but there are so many written accounts of his work that it's easy to get a sense of his authenticity and of the effect he had on those who were present.

The chemist and physicist Sir William Crookes conducted a series of experiments on Home, and it is said that these tests were in fact set up to destroy the medium's reputation, yet the eminent man of science's findings, published in the *Quarterly Journal of Science* in the summer of 1871, were entirely in favour of Home. Never having seen this paper, I can only imagine how convincing the messages and evidence must have been. Sir William Crookes himself commented that what he experienced should have been 'impossible to the rational mind', but none the less did happen.

I asked one of my own sons, whom I consider to be quite intelligent, to research some of the old mediums for me, and two minutes into his Google search he told me, 'Dad, that D. D. Home was a total fraud, according to Wikipedia.' I asked him to do more searches and see what he came up with. In the morning I got up and found that he had stayed up all night researching D. D. Home and had been completely fascinated by what he had read. He had been so gripped that he hadn't even moved on to another medium on the list.

What I'm saying is that today most people go on the internet and accept the first things they see in front of them, as was the case with my son. He hadn't been willing to put in the effort, but I think now I can consider him to be quite the expert on the life of this phenomenal medium. This is because he dug deeper into the information available and looked at it from different angles. It's always worth taking the time to do this.

Exceptional as he was, D. D. Home didn't give a lot of detailed messages to people in the way that the mediums who have followed him have done. There were times when short sentences might be whispered in the séance room, giving names or small pieces of evidence to sitters, but the focus was more on sensational events that defied the laws of physics.

All in all, I believe that the spirit world was experimenting in its use of Home and other early mediums in an attempt to hone the different gifts of mediumship. It was almost as if Home was a prototype, one that displayed every faculty of mediumship and paranormal activity. Over the years, people attending his séances – who, in total, numbered thousands – witnessed a complete repertoire of mediumistic occurrences, too many to be fake.

If we look at the mediums who followed Home in the early twentieth century, we can see their abilities began to be refined and to become more focused on a particular discipline – for instance, what became known as direct voice mediumship, where the independent voices of spirits would be heard in a séance. This was also the time when people began to report seeing the substance known as ectoplasm or telleplasm, a white substance that would be exuded from the body of an entranced medium and would take the form of a spirit person, who would then converse with loved ones at the séance.

Truth or Trickery?

Physical mediumship was always followed by controversy, because it was almost always practised in a completely dark room or in some cases a room lit only by a very dim red light, and this led sceptics to cry fraud all over the place. In many cases they had cause, because for every genuine exponent of physical mediumship, there were usually ten tricksters.

By the 1880s there were an estimated 8 million Spiritualists in the United States and Europe. The Fox sisters were under a lot of strain to produce phenomena and both Maggie and Kate turned to drink. On 21 October 1888, in an interview with the magazine *New York World* for which she was very well paid, Maggie claimed that they had initially created the raps and other noises by means of an apple on a string and later by cracking their knuckles and toe joints. She recanted this confession a year later, and many people were left not knowing what to believe.

It is very hard to believe an account of a physical event if you weren't there when it happened. It is so easy to think that it is made up, but if there is a message there and it includes information that the people involved couldn't have known at the time, then it's worth looking at.

As a medium myself, I certainly don't believe everything I read about the old practices and have actually found myself laughing out loud at some of the pictures that were taken at so-called séances where people gathered together around a table in the dark to contact spirits.

I'm not saying, however, that physical mediumship was just trickery rather than a demonstration of genuine spiritual phenomena. I am often asked if I have ever witnessed physical phenomena like ectoplasm, direct voice mediumship or levitation, and the fact is I have. During the thirty years or so I've spent developing my gifts, I have seen spirits appear – admittedly not through the build-up of ectoplasm, but by forming out of light, almost like holograms – and have often heard independent voices speak too.

In fact, it would appear that I demonstrated some form of physical mediumship in my first ever encounter with the world of the unseen spirits, though it was less noisy than that of the Fox sisters. I have told this story many times, so will just recap it briefly here.

I was just seven years old and was playing on my own in the small front garden outside our home in Glasgow when I saw a man walking towards me from the far end of our street. He was called Ummy and I knew him well. In fact, he had been my late grandmother's live-in partner, something children my age would never have been told in those days, so to me he was just a good friend of my mum and dad.

Ummy was a jolly man and, as he got close to me, I could make out his smiling face and hear him singing a happy song, which seemed to echo through my head: 'We will be buried in Dalbeth, we will be buried in Dalbeth.' He looked so bright and happy that I began to sing along, and I wanted to run towards him, but my feet were somehow rooted to the spot. Then I became aware that he was moving slowly backwards in the direction he had come from, still smiling and waving at me. I heard him say goodbye and then he finally disappeared out of sight.

I ran indoors to tell my mother what had happened, but to my astonishment she shouted at me and told me to stop telling lies.

Sometime later I learned that Ummy had died just over a week or so earlier and my parents had buried him in a cemetery in the east end of Glasgow called Dalbeth. All they could afford was a pauper's grave, and my mother was so upset and embarrassed about this that she and my father hadn't told anyone about it. She eventually said to me that on reflection she hoped that Ummy had come back that day to say that he was happy and that none of that material stuff mattered. I can say that he seemed happy to have been buried in Dalbeth and I'm sure he'd have wanted my mother and father to know that, so his message from the other side was positive and in some ways helpful to two people who had cared for him in the best way they could.

'I Swear I Saw This Happen'

During my search of physical mediums who stood out from the rest, I came across a Welsh medium called Jack Webber. Though he was operating decades after the heyday of physical mediumship, he was able to produce physical manifestations and direct voice mediumship during his séances in the 1930s, until his early death in 1940, at the age of thirty-three.

In a 1939 report on one of his séances, which featured in a two-page spread in the newspaper the *Sunday Pictorial*, the journalist was so taken aback by what he experienced that he prefaced his report with an affidavit saying:

> *I, Bernard Gray, of 27 Barn Rise, Wembley Park, in the county of Middlesex, journalist, make Oath and say as follows. That my description of the incidents enumerated in the article written by me hereunto annexed and marked 'B. G.' to appear in the issue of the Sunday Pictorial of the Twenty-eighth day of May*

One Thousand nine hundred and thirty-nine under the heading of 'I Swear I Saw This Happen' is true. I further make Oath and say that incidents so described in such Article did occur in my presence.

In the article he describes how after tying the medium to a chair, he watched, along with the thirteen other people in the séance, as a range of phenomena began to take place. In the dim red light a face appeared, made from what could only be described as ectoplasm. It built up slowly, first forming features like eyelids and cheekbones, and it did not look white, as a ghost might, but fully human, with a healthy skin tone. To his surprise, he recognised it as the face of an old lady he knew. She then spoke to him and gave her exact name, which no one else at the séance knew. She told him that she couldn't stay long, but she wanted him and the others gathered to see her. Her face then moved around the room, letting all the sitters witness it. Other phenomena continued for ninety minutes.

Jack Webber gave convincing séances like this in the ten or eleven years he practised as a medium and many people testified that they not only believed what they witnessed to have been real, but to have provided evidence of the continuation of the spirit after physical death.

A Pantomime in the Dark

Unfortunately, not every medium provides such convincing phenomena. I have witnessed fraudulent mediums over the years and can truly say that what they demonstrated by way of phenomena any magician could easily have staged.

I recall being asked to attend a séance of physical mediumship back in 1995 and remember feeling quite excited by the
thought of the phenomena I might witness.

The first thing we were all asked to do was take off any
metal jewellery, which we would get back at the close of
the event. It was said that metal in a séance might lead to
chemical reactions which might cause damage to the
medium.

Then we sat in a circle and were told to hold hands and
continue this all the way through the two-hour session.

Next, we all sang songs, led by one of the organisers, to
build a positive vibration and allow the medium, who was
sitting separately, to go off into a trance. I had witnessed
many sessions of trance mediumship by this time and during
that séance I never felt the atmosphere change the way it
normally did when a spirit took control of a medium, but I
kept an open mind.

Before long, two luminous cones, or 'trumpets', which had
been placed in the centre of the circle, seemed to be levitating
and moving around the group. In the old direct voice circles,
trumpets like this were used to amplify the spirit voices, but
during this séance no voices came from them. The medium
who was supposed to be in a trance did, however, speak in
a different voice from his own and called out messages to
people in the group by name – for example, 'George, your
wife is here. She is happy now and she doesn't want you to
be sad any more.' At that point, a man called George, who
I later learned was one of the best friends of the medium,
began to cry loudly.

More messages came for people the medium knew and
they all made a bit of a fuss and became very emotional,
causing others to call out sympathetic words to them, like

'Oh, don't be sad – you heard your wife say she was happy now.'

The only thing about this was the spirits themselves never spoke, as was supposed to happen at a séance like this; instead, all the messages came through the medium. The point of us building all this supposed positive energy in dark conditions was to make the communication stronger and more direct, but this never happened. From time to time a famous medium was said to be coming through and talking about their life, only nothing of any significance was ever said.

I must admit that I was very disappointed. Even the atmosphere in the room was heavy and dull; there was no spiritual feeling in the session and nothing like the evidence that was given in the old direct voice séances of mediums like John Sloan and Etta Wriedt, who both gave exact names and important, relevant information to sitters.

Just in case this had been a poor night, I attended two more of this type of séance in the 1990s, but then I gave up, as they all seemed to involve the same series of non-evidential events, and other than trumpets flying around a darkened room, which any accomplice could have made happen, I saw nothing out of the ordinary and found it all a waste of time.

I had always thought that if we created conducive conditions for spirits, they could produce astounding physical phenomena and information, and I'm sure they did when the genuine mediums of the past worked with them. Sadly, today there honestly isn't anyone I could recommend who is still doing this type of mediumship. There might be someone out there doing it but, if so, they are keeping it very quiet. The stuff that I sat through would never have stood up to the scrutiny of the scientists and other intelligent people who investigated the old mediums. In fact, it was just a pantomime in the dark.

Modern Telekinesis

Having said all this, however, I have witnessed telekinesis, where physical objects move on their own, three times in front of other witnesses.

One of those occasions was during a private reading I was doing for a young widow and her teenage son at their home on the outskirts of Glasgow in 1998. Her husband, who had been killed in a tragic car accident several years earlier, came through and gave very accurate evidence of his continued existence. He was able to tell me that his name was Sam, where and when he had died, and even the type and colour of the sports car he had been driving.

After some fifteen minutes of the reading, I heard him telling me that he always gave his wife a rose on Valentine's Day and on her birthday, which was coming up in a few days, and as I shared this with the woman, the atmosphere in the room became very intense. She and her son could obviously feel this too, as they both shuddered as if chilled to the bone by a cold wind, though the room was warm.

It was right at that moment that an independent voice spoke from the top corner of the room, near the ceiling, saying, 'Sam.'

The three of us looked up at that point and then back at one another in amazement as a red rose raised itself up from a vase of flowers on the table between us and seemed to hover for maybe two or three seconds before dropping in front of the lady, who was sitting directly opposite me.

As well as the chill in the room, I then noticed that I couldn't feel my body below my neck. I wasn't disturbed by that, because when I sat in meditation in my development group, the idea was to go into a trance state, and the way I was feeling resembled that state. It very rarely happened to me during a reading, though, so that was somewhat surprising.

There was a moment of total quiet as we all took in what had just happened, and then the son laughed out loud and said, 'That was Dad, wasn't it?'

I could only agree.

From that day to this, I have never experienced anything quite like that again, although other strange things have taken place when the two worlds come together.

The most 'phenomenal' sight I ever witnessed happened in the early days of my spiritual development. I was about twenty-five at the time and living with my wife and two small sons in the north of Glasgow. It was an ordinary Sunday and I remember that my wife and I were playing with the children when there was a loud bang and clatter at the letterbox. When I went to the door, there were two small kids standing there, both shouting excitedly that I should come to their home, that their dad wanted me now, and that it was very important.

I knew who they were. Their mother, a neighbour of ours, had been killed in a tragic road accident a week earlier.

I remember how the little girl, aged about nine, grabbed my hand and pulled me with her as her younger brother tore off ahead of us in the direction of their flat, which was on the first floor of the tenement block on the corner of our street.

As we reached the open door of the flat, I saw their father standing at the far end of the long hallway leading into the living room. He waved me into the house.

Entering the living room, I noticed that two neighbours were there too. I began to enquire why I had been sent for, but before anyone could answer, the little girl called out that it was happening again.

Even as she spoke, I could hear tapping noises coming from what seemed like the walls and floor of the living room, and as I looked around in wonder I became aware that everyone else was doing the same.

It was the father of the children who spoke first, saying to the neighbours that he had told them so, he hadn't been hammering, and the noise was 'just happening'.

There we were, six people in a small living room, three adults and two children, listening to spirit raps. My mind went straight to what I had read about the Fox sisters and other mediums of the nineteenth century, and I sent out a thought to the mother of the children, saying, 'If this is you, rap twice.'

Two very loud raps sounded instantly. I also became aware of the woman's presence in the room with us.

This was before I was practising as a medium, but it was known in the local area that I attended the Spiritualist church, so the father asked me if this had anything to do with his wife. That was why he had called me to the house.

I was about to explain that I could feel the spirit lady's presence when something happened that I will never forget. The carpet we were standing on, which was nailed tight to the floor, lifted in what I can only describe as a wave of energy, and all of us, and the furniture in the room, were raised off the floor. It wasn't frightening – if anything, there was an amazing feeling of joy all around us. I know this sounds hard to believe, but it honestly happened just as I describe it now.

The children started laughing and the adults smiling, and then it came to an end and all the adults went to the edge of the carpet to examine it and found it was still nailed tightly to the floor.

Then, just beside my left ear I could clearly hear the voice of the mother talking to me – probably more clearly than I had ever heard a spirit voice before in my life. It was as if I was listening to a person talking on a very clear phone line. I looked at the other people who were present, because the communication was so loud that I assumed they were hearing what I was, but no, it seemed that it was just me. She was, though, eager to let her husband and children know that she was still close to them.

I didn't want to speak out in front of everyone, so I said nothing, but as I stood there, the carpet lifted again. Over the next few minutes, the phenomenon was repeated several times.

The neighbours eventually left, quite bewildered by it all, and I had the chance to give the message to the family. At the end of it I was aware that the atmosphere in the room had changed. When I had entered, there had been a highly charged feeling in the place, but this had now been replaced by a calm, the likes of which I can only say would be experienced right after a hurricane.

As with so many people who try to explain very bizarre happenings, I just cannot account for how it took place. I remember the neighbour pulling at the nailed-down edge of the carpet and shaking his head in total disbelief. We all knew what we had experienced, but had something very paranormal taken place or had it been a mass hallucination?

My own feeling now, as I look back at this event, was that the power of the mother's love for her family caused all the phenomena. I know the very detailed message of love and hope definitely came from her.

I remember that some years later, when I was doing research for a book that was to be written about my friend Albert Best, I came across a Catholic priest from Glasgow who told me that he had once been invited to watch Albert give a session of mediumship to a small group of people in a friend's house, and in the middle of the messages he and everyone in the room had witnessed the chair Albert was sitting in being raised off the floor. Though Albert protested, telling the spirits to put him down, the priest described the atmosphere in the room as being one of immense joy and happiness. He said he had never felt anything like it before.

An interesting point to note is that a lady who was present at that séance was given an incredibly accurate message full of hope and healing from her husband, who had been dead less than two weeks. This was similar to my case, where the mother of the children had died very recently. In fact, her funeral had been the day before.

As I said earlier, it is very hard to believe an account of physical phenomena if you weren't there at the time. It is so easy to think that everything has been made up, or that the witness is deluded, or was when it happened. All I can really say is to look at the witness and consider why they might be telling such a tale. Is it for attention? Were other witnesses present? Are there any other factors that might explain what happened?

The other thing to note here is that in both of the above cases the people died very untimely deaths – a speeding car hit the mother, and the husband at Albert's séance had died in a tragic accident at work. It makes me wonder whether there is a stronger spirit force available to communicate when people are taken like this. This might even explain the dramatic paranormal events that happen in wartime, when there is so much sudden death and intense emotion. Who knows?

I will look at the events of wartime in a later chapter, but first I would like to outline some more ways in which spirits can communicate with us and how we can assess the validity of the messages.

3

Communication with Spirits and Guides

The dramatic phenomena of physical mediumship certainly drew a lot of attention and established the idea of spirit communication in people's minds, whether they accepted it was possible or not.

As time moved on, however, other methods came more to the fore. It was as if the spirit world was refining the ways of communicating and presenting what was suitable for the current level of human consciousness. As the twentieth century progressed, spirit messages became more detailed and personal, so it was often up to the individual concerned to decide whether to accept them or not. Similarly, mediums progressed from using outer displays of paranormal phenomena to the inner skills of clairvoyance, clairaudience and clairsentience, where pictures, sounds and feelings are used to describe the spirits who are communicating. This is known as 'mental mediumship'.

Clairvoyance

Both mediums and psychics can be clairvoyant – i.e. see images of either a person's life or, in the case of the medium, the life of a person in the spirit world.

One twentieth-century medium who was known for giving

detailed visual images in all his messages was Gordon Higginson, from Staffordshire. He first publicly demonstrated his mediumship on his twelfth birthday and did so for another sixty-three years. He was a real showman, but an excellent clairvoyant and mental medium.

I heard that in one message on the platform for the Glasgow Association of Spiritualists in the 1960s, he told a woman in the audience that he could see her father and he described what he had looked like before he died. He then went on to describe a picture that had been taken of her father when he'd been in the forces and said that the lady had that very photograph in her handbag. This was demonstrably true, and the lady produced it from her bag.

Gordon then described her house, giving details of every room before telling her that her father watched her walk through the house every night, crying about how empty her life was, and was encouraging her to look at what she still had and not at how alone she felt.

This is not only a good example of clairvoyant communication, but also of a message where proof is given, then words of hope encourage the recipient to go forward in their life.

Clairaudience

Messages can also come through clairaudience, where mediums hear the voices and sounds of spirit.

One medium who stood out for her great ability to hear spirits was Helen Hughes, who came from the north east of England. At the height of her mediumship, from the 1930s to the 1960s, this sprightly, rather frail little woman often stood in front of audiences of thousands of people and mystified them with her incredibly accurate quick-fire style of spirit communication. When I hear people tell me stories of messages they received from her, I am totally inspired.

Albert Best told me that he'd met her in the early 1950s and been greatly impressed by a message she'd given to a woman in the audience at the Spiritualist Association of Great Britain (SAGB) in London. Helen had actually singled out the woman Albert had brought down with him from Scotland. Her name was Cathy Clarke and she had lost her eighteen-year-old son in a car accident months before. As she was close to Albert, he wanted her to have a reading with a medium who wouldn't know anything about her circumstances.

Helen told her that a young man was standing behind her and was saying his name was John, but he was known as Junior. This was correct. She gave the date he died and told Cathy he was sorry that he had never got to say goodbye to her. Albert told me that this was something Cathy had kept saying – that she wished she could have said goodbye to her son.

Helen then told her that Junior was with Grandpa Jack and Mrs Todd. This was very good evidence, because Jack was his grandfather who had died when he was ten and Mrs Todd was Jack's partner, though in those days such a thing wouldn't have been mentioned and she was always known to Junior as Mrs Todd. She had only passed a year earlier.

The message ended with Helen telling Cathy that Junior was laughing about the fact that she had chosen an angel statue for his grave, because in reality he was no angel. This was again true, but it was Helen's final words that impressed Albert most: 'Now you can cancel your reading, your son says, but he will come to you again.' Helen had not known that Albert had booked a reading for Cathy.

In this reading accurate clairvoyance and clairaudience were displayed. Here are two more examples of how brilliant Helen's clairaudient abilities were, taken from the small book *The Mediumship of Helen Hughes* (SDU Publication, 2006), which has some of the verbatim accounts of her amazing messages from the spirit world and gives some idea of her style of delivery:

> *In 1939 at a public demonstration in Leeds:*
>
> *Helen, pointing to a woman in the audience, 'Is your name Nelly?'*
>
> *'Yes,' the woman answers.*
>
> *Helen: 'Well then, you knew Mr Bramwell, and I have to tell you that he is here and he has brought Harry and Mrs Wilson. She says she's alright now, and thanks you for what you did for her. She tells me that she suffered from a weak heart. She also tells me that your name is Boynton.'*
>
> *'Yes, this is all correct.'*

This type of message is short, sharp, very accurate and right to the point. There is no fishing for answers in Helen's mediumship and the message of thanks is conveyed from the spirit without fuss.

* * *

*At a public meeting at Gateshead
on September 27, 1936:*

Helen: 'There is a young woman here named Eva,
who was a musician.' This was claimed by two
people. Singling out one of them, she said, 'You are
Eva's mother. She tells me she played the piano and
she had a companion called Elsie who has also passed
over. Her full name is Eva Huxley. I also get the
name of Margaret Murrit and she is calling out
"Fragile!" She shows me a hamper with "Fragile"
written on it and though she is Maggie she says that
when she was a baby you put her in the hamper
and called her "Fragile" and the name stuck to her
for some time. Is that so?'

'Yes.'

'She now tells me that you have been to the cemetery
today, and she was with you when you stood at
the grave and wept. She says you are not to do
it. You have heard knockings in the house and
you have several times got out of bed and gone to
look for them. They have made you nervous. You
have nothing to fear – it is only your daughter
knocking.'

All of what she told the woman was totally accepted
as being correct.

This type of mediumship is quite magnificent and anybody
who saw Mrs Hughes work could testify that she always
worked in this no-nonsense way, giving exact first and second

names and sometimes even addresses to her recipients, no matter what town or city she was working in. It might be suggested that she had accomplices planted among the audience, but it would be ludicrous to assume that she took ten to twenty people with her all over the country, and other countries, just to cheat that well. From the details she gave, we would have to assume that this lady was the real deal.

In the two messages above you will note that as well as clairaudience there was also the faculty of clairvoyance at work when Helen mentioned that she was being shown the hamper marked 'Fragile'. This tells us that she was using more than one faculty of mediumship at the same time. The way she describes it tells me that she was seeing the image in her thinking mind, a kind of subjective vision, unlike the more physical way I saw Ummy, and this type of vision often complements clairaudience.

Helen was a brilliant exponent of spirit communication and I will refer to her work again later on, but for now I would like to move on to clairsentience.

Clairsentience

Many mediums have the gift of clairsentience: the ability to feel or sense things in the atmosphere around them. I have experienced it myself. It's a sense of knowing there's 'something different' going on. In some instances, a medium might experience feelings that those in the spirit world have actually experienced themselves and through this can convey messages or even warnings.

We all have the ability to feel spirit in a 'sixth-sensory' way, beyond the five senses of sight, sound, taste, smell and touch, often when we're least expecting it. I honestly don't recall how many times I've heard people tell me that they were doing chores and thinking of nothing important when they felt a presence standing behind them or in the room with them.

The thing is, just as with spirit visions or voices, the moment we focus on what's happening, we come out of the moment and lose the connection. This can make it difficult to evaluate, because as soon as we start to think about it, it's gone! Then logic tells us not to be stupid and that we've imagined it, but I have to say that it is very difficult to imagine a presence. That's why we remember such occasions and experiences, yet file them in our mind under 'strange but true'. It's usually only when people reveal that they've had similar experiences that we feel safe to share our own 'strange but true' files.

If you've ever felt an overwhelming sense of presence and wondered what was happening, maybe I can make it a little clearer for you. As a medium who has become used to such things and thinks nothing of them, I have learned that when I feel a spirit presence it is because my thinking mind is on slow-down – that is, I am meditating, or daydreaming, or preparing to open up to the spirit to demonstrate my mediumship. When this happens, I feel my own light body or aura vibrating around my physical body. In the early days this would resemble palpitations around my chest, and this is why people who experience this type of thing randomly or as a one-off get startled by it. But the more common it becomes, the easier it is to recognise that the quickening feeling is the separation of the two bodies and, when this occurs, you are in a state of mind to sense the two worlds or realities, the spirit world and this one.

I recall the very moment when this became clear to me. It happened when I was in my late twenties and I was practising meditation and developing my abilities as a medium.

I had returned home from my meditation class one night and sat down on a chair in my living room to go over in my mind what had happened in the class. I remember that my body felt very relaxed and that my thoughts were very quiet inside my head. For a moment I found it hard to create any more thoughts and yet at the same time I was becoming more aware of the room I was sitting in, though my eyes were now closed. There followed the feeling of my heart beating faster, and even though I was relaxed and stationary, it felt as though the chair was moving and vibrating. Then the pounding of my heart was no more and it felt as though *I* was the vibration and I had expanded beyond my body and the chair and was filling the room.

At the same moment I became aware of a friend of mine who had not long died. I didn't see him, but felt that I knew everything he was feeling, and that lifted me to another level, beyond the room and any thoughts of anything physical or material. I sensed many other spirits I knew, but time now had no bearing and I felt as though I was buzzing and was more enlightened than I had ever been. There was an amazing sense of lightness and expansion, but no sense of limitation. Even now my words cannot explain what the experience contained.

I came out of it with one deep intake of breath and felt jolted forward in my chair. My eyes opened, but my vision was out of focus for a couple of seconds or so. I remember looking at the clock on the wall above my fireplace and it showed that two hours had passed. To my mind, it could only have been seconds. It was amazing and incredible all at the same time, and my body felt as though it was filled with electricity – a sensation I'd never known before.

I had had a proper out-of-body experience, where my light body had separated from my physical one, and because of this I learned that even in a less extreme separation, such as going in or coming out of sleep, or even daydreaming, there must be a loosening of the connection between the two bodies, and this is why some people experience the presence of loved ones in the spirit world just for a moment. When this happens, it's not because they're coming to tell you something, it is more to do with you going out to them. If they are close to you, then you may experience the feeling of being with them.

Waking Up Our Mind

Spirits can actually communicate with us easily, I would say, but we need to wake up our mind to receive their messages. Otherwise doubt will block the communication.

There are many times when people dream of their loved ones in spirit, and although this can be to do with memory and emotions, spirits can communicate with us when we are in a semi-sleep state because our mind is open and logic is resting. When this truly happens, we tend to know, and to consider it is more of an encounter than a dream. This is usually because there is a vibrational quality to the experience and also that the message makes perfect sense. Communication like this is very subjective, but what is key is looking at the evidence in the message.

The same can be said for synchronistic events that occur repeatedly and that we associate with a loved one in the spirit world. Such an event might be the finding of a certain object, often in places it shouldn't be, especially just after we have been thinking of our loved one. This could be the spirit person's way of letting us know that they are there.

Another way that a spirit can remind us that they are close to us is through the sense of smell. I think that if we were to conduct a study into this phenomenon, millions of people would admit to having smelled a scent which reminded them of a loved one, perhaps a particular perfume they wore, or the stench of tobacco, or just their own personal scent.

Our loved ones in the spirit world sometimes try to catch our attention by appearing to us, but we have to be in an altered state of consciousness to see them, so we might be thinking of nothing in particular and catch a glimpse of them just slightly out of focus, usually out of the corner of our eye. Many people have reported that they have seen someone just at the edge of their peripheral vision, only to look straight at them and find no one is there, yet they can't help feeling otherwise.

A similar experience can be had with hearing the voice of a loved one when daydreaming, or even when concentrating on one single thing. Once again spirit can reach us when our mind isn't looking for them and our rational mind is resting.

The fact that the rational mind has to be put to one side means there will always be sceptics and doubters, and it can be difficult for other people to evaluate these experiences, but I am sure that spirits are attracting our attention and reminding us of their love in these and many more ways.

With some mediums, spirits even use many of their faculties and speak through them directly. This is known as 'trance mediumship'.

Trance Mediumship

Trance mediumship has been around as long as humanity and is often performed in tribal cultures by shamans or oracles. In the Spiritualist movement, trance mediumship occurs when the conscious mind of a medium is dialled down, a bit like using a dimmer switch on a light. When this happens, a spirit can use the mind and voice of the medium to communicate directly with people. Unlike mental mediumship, which is often used for personal sittings, trance mediumship is usually done in public, or small private groups.

Once Spiritualism had become a popular movement, trance mediums seemed to turn up and demonstrate their abilities all over the place, not only allowing spirits to speak through them but even producing physical manifestations and feats of telekinesis. People who wonder why this type of mediumship is not so common today would get their answer by asking the mediums of old how long they sat in their development circles. I'm sure they would soon see why. Too many people want to develop mediumship today in a very short space of time, and that is sad, because the length of time you spend building a link to the spirit world is the foundation of your mediumship, and I do believe that if a medium has the proper training, trust in spirit and discipline in the early days, they can develop trance mediumship. I sat under my teacher Mrs Primrose's guidance for five full years before working as a medium and then another two to build up my connection to spirit enough to gain the ability to do trance, so really it was a seven-year apprenticeship. In the words of my teacher, 'If you want to be a good medium, you had better put in the time.'

Once again I must point out that for every genuine trance

medium, there were always charlatans who play-acted for monetary gain or for some other sort of success. I think in the case of the old physical and trance mediums, those who were genuine not only produced unbelievable happenings, but there was a purpose to them, and that was to convince grieving people of the continued existence of their loved one, not to put on a show. That's how you can tell the difference. I can always remember Mrs Primrose telling me that when it comes to séances, 'If it looks like a show, then it probably is.'

Francis John, the Brightest Star in the Sky

Most mediumship today is mental mediumship, although there are still some mediums, though very few, who can produce messages in trance states. I recall that when I first began to practise as a medium, I always worked as a mental medium, giving messages to congregations in Spiritualist churches, and always remaining very lucid and aware of what was happening. It was in one of the very early private readings I gave, to a family outside Glasgow, that all changed for me and my mediumship moved on to a very different level.

I was working as a barber at the time in a small salon in the west end of the city and I got a call at my work from a lady asking me if I would come to her home and help her family, who had just suffered a loss. Her name was Mrs Preston, she told me, and she gave me the address I could go to when I had time to see them. I can still recall the sadness in her voice and my heart told me that I would have to answer this call for help.

The following day was my day off and I decided to go

and see Mrs Preston and try to help her. I arrived at the train station and was picked up by her husband, who told me nothing about the loss they had suffered. Instead we shared small talk in the couple of minutes it took me to walk to the flat where they lived.

I remember on meeting Mrs Preston how her eyes seemed so big and brown and full of sorrow that I knew I had to try my best to bring some joy back to this broken life.

As I always do at the beginning of a reading like this, I told her what might happen if I got a contact and that it would just be as simple as a conversation between us. She seemed to be so tense that I asked her to put her hand in mine.

I had no sooner touched her hand than I heard the voice of a young man saying, 'Mum, Mum, I'm here.' I passed this information to her and then I clearly heard a name in my left ear, as if someone was standing close beside me, whispering, 'Francis John.'

When I mentioned this, tears ran down the woman's face and then I honestly had no feeling in my body for a moment and I could feel myself going into a trance state – exactly what I had told Mrs Preston wouldn't happen.

I will let her tell you what happened next:

I had never had a sitting with a medium before. When Gordon entered my home, I was a bit taken aback by how young he was. I had really expected someone older. However, once he spoke to me and settled my fears, I felt quite safe in his hands.

Gordon took my hand and then said that the words 'Mum, I'm here' had come through, after which he told me my son's proper name, Francis John, which _is what he was christened, although he was known to us as Franky._

Gordon said at the outset that he wouldn't go into a funny trance, but that's exactly what he did. When his eyes closed, he remained quiet for a while and then a voice quite different from his own spoke through him.

I was told that my son was safe and that he hadn't felt a thing when he had passed away. I was then told the exact date he had died, which was ten days earlier. It then became clear that he was influencing the voice that was speaking, as it said things in a way that only he could.

My heart began to fill with joy as the discourse continued. Franky had been married for just over a year when the tragedy struck. His young widow was called Christine. During the session he said, 'Tell Chris to remember the Lake District.' This was where they had their honeymoon. He then sent his regards to the rest of the family, calling each by their first name.

The information that came through to me was all relevant to the life of my son and the life of my family.

At the end of the session, Franky told me if I ever wanted to see him I should look up to the brightest star in the sky. This was what I would say to him when he was a child and asked where his grandpa had gone after he died. I always said to him, 'Look for the brightest star in the sky, Franky. That is where your grandpa is.'

I don't know what prompted me to have a sitting with a medium, but what I do know is that I have spoken directly with my son in heaven and he sounded so happy. I thank this young man for his special gift and ask God

to look after him, so that he may bring happiness to
many others who have suffered as our family has.
(Gordon Smith, *Spirit Messenger,* Hay House 2003)

That sitting took place back in 1992, when I was thirty, but I did look young for my age, and now when I read back over it, I'm not surprised that Mrs Preston, never having had a sitting with a medium before, probably thought they would be older and maybe have a particular sort of look.

Thinking back to that time, I had no idea that I would be used in that way to bring through a contact, but the results were quite profound. In trance communication, the information becomes much more direct, as there is no interference from the mind of the medium. Whenever this happens to me now, I just let go and allow it to happen, as I have learned to trust the process and know that my spirit guide, Chi, knows better than I do what will help the sitter most.

Spirit Guides – Helpers or Fantasy Figures?

Spiritualism has no main deity or figure of worship at the centre of its teachings, but from its early beginnings, mediums spoke about their spirit guides, or guardians of a higher realm of the spirit world, who watched over them and directed and developed their gifts. Each individual who practised in Spiritualist churches had the opportunity to find their own spiritual teacher in the form of a guide, and this was something that was quite appealing to many people who were turning away from the authoritarian structures of orthodox religion.

The guides in this early time always seemed to take the

form of Native Americans or wise oriental teachers and gurus. Some mediums even claimed that their guides were characters from the Bible or other religious texts.

When I was in my own development circle, I wanted to have a Native American as a guide, just like the great mediums of the past, but when I was growing up, these people meant little or nothing to me other than being part of the cowboy and Indian films I watched on television. I had never really been brought up with a Christian background either, and my only connection to religious thinking was to the wise Chinese masters I had read about in books on martial arts or seen on TV shows about Kung Fu. So it seemed quite natural to me that when I asked to see an image of my spirit guide he would appear as an old wise oriental master. That's what I assumed a spiritual teacher would look like.

As a young boy, I would also sometimes see a girl around my own age whom no one else could see. She seemed to appear to me when I felt sad or frightened by things that were going on in my family at the time. She always made me feel calm and if she appeared in my darkened room at night I would find that it would be easy to fall asleep and let go of my concerns. She also seemed to be a spirit guide of sorts.

Now, this idea of individual spirit guides is all fine and good when a person is of sound mind and is grounded and, if practising mediumship, is doing so from a balanced mind. The problem arises when people who are extreme in their beliefs begin to fantasise and create images as a result of their own desire.

I have known many Spiritualists who have become fixated on a historical hero and then believed them to be their guide. There was one man I watched demonstrating his so-called trance mediumship at Glasgow University before Professor Roy. A physics teacher in his day job, he believed that his guide was the great British physicist Sir Oliver Lodge. He made the claim that his guide could transfer the sound of a human voice onto magnetic tape if the tape were placed in his hands during the trance. He brought an assistant with him who just so happened to have a sealed blank tape with her and then he went into his trance (or, as Archie politely put it, 'shallow altered state'), but before she could place the tape in his hands, the professor, who had seen him do this sort of thing in other demonstrations, produced his own tape from his top pocket and placed that in his hands instead. Obviously when it was played back, it was still blank.

People like this can become totally obsessed by the idea of a spirit guide and can delude themselves about the role of the imaginary guide in their everyday life. In this respect, they are no different from people of the same mentality who have religious convictions. Some extremely religious people believe that they have a direct line to God and even think that God talks to them every day of their life and gives them direction. We don't have to look too far back in history, or even in today's society, to see the trouble that religious extremists can cause and the horrific acts they can carry out in the name of their religion.

Spiritualism is different in this respect from other religions, because it can be tested to some extent rather than simply accepted on the basis of faith. A trance medium allowing their guide to speak through them, for example, could use the evidence that they received in their messages to validate the existence of a higher mind at work through them. The feedback would show that it wasn't just a strong belief at work, but a consciousness which had information that the recipient had not yet acquired. The medium could therefore build up trust in the guide, and when they delivered teachings rather than messages, people would be able to trust that they were true.

Many will ask why a medium should have to go into a trance to allow the voice of a guide to speak through them when the same result could be obtained using telepathy between the spirit and the medium. The idea, I believe, is that in such cases the medium feels separate from the information and the spirit can demonstrate a separate personality that has access to information beyond human knowledge. This also stops people from believing that mediums are saintly or special. Mediums are not meant to become objects of other people's worship, and even the guides claim to be gaining the knowledge from a source higher than they.

So, in effect, a spirit guide is a go-between in the spirit world, a key to higher wisdom and knowledge. Mediums of the old days would often say that they were merely instruments of spirit, or channels, and so on, and it was true. If a housewife with no great education, like Helen Hughes, could speak to learned men when in a trance state and surprise them with incredibly intelligent information about things they assumed she could never know, she couldn't be the source of the information, merely a conduit. The logical conclusion would be that the higher mind of the spirit was of higher intelligence than the human one.

As I continued to develop my mediumship and my understanding of spirit, it became clear to me that the higher mind of spirit could take on any form that a medium required in order to get them to raise their vibration to a more spiritual way of thinking. So it is my belief that spirit guides appear to people in the form of archetypes that will command their respect, but to all intents and purposes they are just aspects of the higher mind of spirit. The spirit girl who appeared to me as a child was the same essence of higher mind as the wise Chinese teacher who became my guide as I got older. The form of a spirit guide is unimportant. It is their love, wisdom and guidance that count.

For me and many other mediums, different figures will appear at different times and the point is to look at the message behind the archetype and learn something from it. For example, a Native American might be there to teach you about the Earth and to respect and value the great world you live in. When you understand this, the image may change to that of a devoted monk or nun, who represents learning about dedication or devotion. I believe it is wise not to assume that every figure you see in meditation is a new guide, but look on them more as opportunities to learn a new aspect of spiritual development.

4

Messages of the Future

At the opening of this book I talked about how many mediums seemed to appear from the middle to the end of the nineteenth century. I consider this as important in the history of mediumship, because it tells me that if the spirit world is the intelligence I believe it to be, and if spirits are privy to future events, then it would make sense that they would be aware of impending wars in this world and preparation would be made to help the people who would be suffering the loss of loved ones *en masse*. But are spirits privy to future events?

Prophecies from Psychics and Mediums

This is a good time to point out that mediums are not fortune-tellers or seers, but there are occasions when a spirit will give information about future events if it is helpful to the recipient. Many seers or psychics predict tragic events and bring bad tidings, which worry or upset a person who receives them, whereas a true medium will work with the sole intention to heal or help the recipient. This is one way to know if a message about the future has come through the psychic gift of second sight or from the spirit world through a medium.

Also, because seers or fortune-tellers often say it like it is with no thought for the effect on the recipient, in many cases they allow their own emotional or mental state to contaminate the prediction with fear. I would even go so far as to say that many seers trip into timelines that have fatalistic outcomes because their own mind is vibrating at a fearful level.

Certainly in the early days of Spiritualism, predictions were given willy-nilly with no thought of the effects on the people who received them. It took many years of psychic investigation into mediumship before mediums were seen to be separate from seers and psychics. Until then, psychic messages from the platform were often still regarded as mediumship.

In one case I read in a book called *That Reminds Me* (Two Worlds Publishing Company, 1938) by a former president of the Spiritualist National Union, a Mr Ernest Oaten, how a Mrs Wilks, described as a rough but kindly soul with a big heart and profound faith in the spirit world, was working as a medium in front of a small gathering in a Yorkshire Spiritualist church in 1912. Mr Oaten says that in the middle of a short but confident talk to the gathering, she suddenly stopped, pointed to a group of several men sitting together in the far corner of the room and said, 'With you men I see a strange sight: flashes of fire, smoke and dust. I'm sure it is an explosion. I'm sure it will happen within the next few days. I do beg you to be careful. I cannot see more details because of the dust.' She then went straight back into her talk as though nothing had happened.

The men were miners and word spread rapidly through the community and a letter was sent out from one of the colliery companies protesting about Spiritualists frightening people and making them nervous at going down the pits. Ernest Oaten was also consulted about the matter.

Some eight days later there was an explosion at Cadeby pit, at the time one of the most up-to-date pits in the country, and a large number of men were killed. One of them was a Mr Richard Wimpenny, one of the group gathered in the Spiritualist church eight days before. A strange thing about this story is that he didn't normally work in that pit, but had only gone in to help them on that day.

Reading this reminds me how far Spiritualism has come, as no medium today who is a member of any recognised organisation would be allowed to make such statements from the platform. I also note from the words used in the account that the medium in question only ever refers to herself in her message rather than mentioning that it is coming from the spirit world, and this again reminds me how unregulated things were back then. I am certain that Mrs Wilks gave many spirit messages in her time, but I also believe that she had some abilities as a seer, and that is clearly how she delivers this prophecy, rather than from her mediumship.

Prophecy that comes from a seer and actually occurs as predicted means that nothing could have been done to stop it. It suggests to me that the seer has seen the end of a timeline that had no chance of continuing, no matter what actions were taken.

Not all timelines are like this. In my experience as a medium, spirits only really offer messages of the future when there is a chance to change or improve a situation.

The absence of future information doesn't mean that there is to be a bad outcome, though; it just means that there are still events to unfold before the future is truly readable.

There are times when I have been asked to give the outcome of a situation and nothing happens. This is not to be seen as an opt-out on the part of the medium, more that the spirit world cannot give any information for one reason or another that might be helpful.

Many times in our lives we would love to know the outcome of a situation we are faced with, but we often do not consider the effect of this when we make such a wish. As a medium, I do not set out to ask for details of a person's future when I deliver a message, but if something comes into the message that belongs to the future, I know that the recipient needs to have the information for some reason, perhaps in order to take a particular step or make a choice that leads to the beginning of a new timeline. In fact, this happened to me.

Timeline Choices

The first person I ever saw demonstrate mediumship in public was a lady called Mary Duffy from Edinburgh. She was very highly regarded as a genuine medium and good public speaker. It was this lovely lady who gave me my first message from the spirit world.

I had gone to the Spiritualist church with my friend Christine, who had just lost her brother, Brian, who had died tragically in a house fire the previous week. I had never been to a Spiritualist meeting before and had no idea what would happen. We sat down on the front row of what could have been a Protestant church and then took part in a religious-type service for a while until the minister asked Mrs Duffy to demonstrate her mediumship.

Then a very bright older lady with short cropped salt and pepper hair spoke to us for a couple of minutes, informing us that she was there to give us information and that we should only say 'yes' or 'no' if she came to us with a message.

Her first port of call was my friend. She told Christine that she didn't have to be a medium to know that she had recently been bereaved, but she told her that her mother was in the spirit world and that she had received the young man who had just gone over, and that she knew that things were very raw, so she would speak to her after the service in private to save any embarrassment.

I remember being very impressed with this because Christine's mother was in the spirit world and, as Christine was only in her early twenties, this wasn't something the medium would have been likely to have picked up from cold reading or reading body language. And the young man who had just gone over would have been Brian. But it was the next thing she said that really blew my mind.

'The young man sitting next to you, darling, I'm sure you know that he is a medium?'

Christine looked round at me and then back at Mrs Duffy in disbelief. She told me later that she was thinking, 'All the true things you've just said and now you go and ruin it with this nonsense!'

But Mrs Duffy continued. 'Yes, this young man actually saw your brother the moment that he died. Hasn't he told you this?'

It was true. I had seen Brian appear in my bedroom in the early hours of the day he died and I'd never told Christine. She'd been so distraught and I really hadn't known whether I should share anything like that with her.

Mrs Duffy then spoke directly to me. 'You are a medium, son, don't you know that?'

I nervously shook my head and she looked straight at me for a moment.

'Well, darling,' she continued, 'I have just been told by your grandmother, who is called Sarah, that you will be standing where I'm standing now doing exactly what I'm doing, and

I think that you'd better have a word with your friend and let her know what you saw.'

It was quite something, I can tell you.

At the end of the service, she gave a second prediction to Christine: 'Darling, I have been told that you will meet the medium called Albert Best and he will give you the message that you need from your brother. This won't happen right away, but it will happen, and I assure you, you will never have a doubt about life after death after that.'

Then she gave me the name of a Mrs Jean Primrose and suggested I went to her church in Glasgow to develop my gift and, as she left, she turned to me and said, 'I'll see you on the platform, darling.'

At that moment, how could I know that Mrs Duffy and I would work together many times?

The interesting thing was that Mrs Duffy wasn't actually the first person to predict the path that lay ahead of me. When I was ten years old I was with my parents one day when they visited an old friend they hadn't seen for many years. This lady brought her sister to meet us and later that day she announced to my parents that I was a clairvoyant and that I would travel the world giving messages to people and that I would write books and teach people about life after death.

Now I mean, who predicts that a child they have never met before will become a medium and travel the world? It's not exactly like saying someone will have a career in the police force or as a chef or something. And I'd certainly never thought of it.

None the less, here I am, and I have now been given so many proofs from the spirit world that time has no bearing on their existence and I believe that they can see us in the here and now and have access to our past and future as well.

It is quite natural to think that accurately predicting future events is supernatural, but have you ever considered how astounding it is to look at an ordinary person and be able to delve into their past and accurately describe episodes from that life? This is something that mediums do so often with the help of spirit.

I also know that some timelines can be changed and that messages from spirit can help to guide us and help us make the best of what may lie ahead. Mrs Duffy saw the road that lay ahead of me and in a way allowed me to take my first step on it.

I often wonder what life would have been like had Christine and I not gone to that church, but I can only assume that I accepted my destiny that night.

Another occasion when I wondered about the relevance of time and choice was when the former president of the Spiritualist Association of Great Britain in London, Stella Blair, with whom I had become great friends, told me about a message she had received from the very well-known medium Mrs Ivy Northage, who often worked at the Association.

Stella hadn't been living in London at the time, but had decided to go for a reading with a medium while she was there because she had come through quite a tough time in her relationship with her partner and was having difficulties in her antiques business. She told me that she felt comfortable with Ivy, who was then in her sixties, as she looked 'just like an ordinary woman'. But then the reading began and Ivy closed her eyes and went into a trance state and spoke in a voice very different from the one in which she had greeted Stella at the beginning.

Stella was shocked when the voice gave her accurate details of her current situation, including the name of her partner, and said she should listen carefully to what was coming next as it would shape her life to come.

At this point of the story, Stella let me hear a tape-recording of the rest of the reading. The voice, which sounded neither male nor female, described the life that was waiting for Stella if she took certain steps. She was told that she would become president of the SAGB and that she would live not more than half a mile from 33 Belgrave Square, where the SAGB was situated. I was actually listening to the recording in her flat, which was about that distance from Belgrave Square, and there were so many other predictions on the tape that I knew had come true, and yet this had all been predicted years earlier, when my friend was at a crossroads in her life. The accuracy of the evidence was quite incredible.

Stella assured me that her past, present and future had been laid out for her in that reading. She had been told that if she took a particular step, all of the things described for her future would come to pass, and when she took that step, they did, and she met her destiny.

This informed me that we often have choice in our life. Not always, but often. For me, it is clear that when we reach the pivotal points on our path where we have to choose, then alternative paths open up to us. In Stella's case, spirits were able to advise and guide her, but she could have refused the advice and gone down another road.

Ivy Northage was a brilliant medium and I am sure that thousands of people who had the opportunity to witness her working in a trance state with her spirit guide communicating through her would have had similar experiences to my friend Stella. I know that she sometimes used her gift to help the police to solve crimes, too, but she, like many other mediums, made very little of this and it is difficult to find much evidence of these cases now that she has gone to the spirit world herself.

A Prediction from a Healer

Going back to my own story, I did contact Mrs Primrose in Glasgow and joined her Thursday evening development circle, where we sat as a group to meditate. She also insisted that each week I attended her healing clinic and had healing sessions with one of her old friends, a nice friendly man then in his early seventies, I would imagine, called John. It was quite strange at first to be asked to receive healing when nothing was wrong with me, but when Mrs Primrose made such a request you never argued with her.

So each Tuesday night I would go to the little Spiritualist church in West Prince's Street in Glasgow and watch the demonstrations of mediumship, and afterwards I would sit on one of the several wooden chairs that were placed around the room and the healers who worked in the church would come and give me and the other people who sat there a session of spiritual healing.

As I mentioned, I honestly had no idea why I was receiving sessions from John, but I went along with it for about six months and each session the same thing would happen: I would sit in the chair and my healer would come and tell me that he wouldn't touch me during the healing, but at the end he would place his hands on my shoulders and that would let me know it was over and I should open my eyes. Each time I would accept this and close my eyes and feel very relaxed, just as I did when I sat in my meditation practice, only there would be times when I would sense a sort of intensity around certain parts of my body, like my forehead or my ears or my solar plexus, and so on.

One night John took me aside and told me that his healing on me was finished now, but I was being prepared for the work that lay ahead of me. I remember wondering what work he was speaking about and thinking to myself that surely it would be a medium who would know such things, not a healer, but he went on, 'Son, you will work as a medium on the platform and you will bring messages to many people around the world. You will have to be psychologically very strong, because many people will challenge what you do, but never worry, because spirit will always be with you when you need them most and you will feel that whenever you take a step up to a higher stage they will prove things at an even deeper level to you.'

I didn't know what to say, because I was a gents' hairdresser and had no intention of travelling the world as a medium, or anything else for that matter.

John then told me that the healing he had been doing on me hadn't been for my physical health, but for my spiritual health. He said that to be a true medium I had to be a clear vessel and the healing he had done was to clear me so that I could channel spirit messages more accurately.

I thanked him and stood there looking puzzled as he walked away.

Then he turned back to look at me and said, 'Oh, and please tell your mother that Sally in the spirit world is looking after her.'

And, with that he went off along West Prince's Street, leaving me with a mind full of questions.

I wondered who Sally was and whether I should tell my mother she was looking after her, because even though my parents now both knew I was going to the Spiritualist church, they were still a bit sceptical about it. I wondered about the world travel, too, and as I sat on the bus on my way home I couldn't see how it could possibly happen.

With all this going round in my head, I decided to call my mother as soon as I got home, because I thought that if the message John had given me for her was true, then, who knew, maybe there would be something to substantiate the rest. I was quite astounded when she said yes, she understood it, and that Sally was her mother. I had grown up thinking that my mother's mother was Sarah, but my mum told me then that those closest to her had called her Sally. I was astounded by this, and equally astounded by the fact that my mother wasn't freaking out at getting a spirit message. In fact, she sounded quite pleased to hear it.

As for the rest of the message, I would just have to wait and see.

Simply the Best

Several months after this episode I was told that one of the greatest mediums of our time was to be giving a demonstration of mediumship at another Spiritualist church in Glasgow. That medium was Albert Best. I was also told that if I wanted to see him I should turn up early, as it would be packed.

I went with two friends, Jim and Karla. We arrived an hour and a half early, and even then we were shocked to see that there was a long line of people all the way to the end of the street. We got the last three seats at the very back of the hall and we waited with pure excitement to see this extraordinary medium do his stuff.

Albert was a short stocky man with fine white hair and would have been in his early seventies then. He had worked in Spiritualist churches and other venues all over the world and there were rumours that he had given readings to anyone who was anyone, so for me as an aspiring medium, this was like watching an idol, only he didn't look like an idol, he was very ordinary and humble in appearance.

When he started his mediumship, I noticed that he spoke in a soft Irish accent, twined with Glaswegian, but it wasn't how he spoke that grabbed me, it was what he said. In his first message he went straight to a woman near the front and said, 'Mrs, your boy is here. He died last year on 7 May from an injury to his head. This man beside you is his father and either you or your boy is called Malcolm.'

The man replied that they were both called by that name.

Albert continued, 'You gave him a silk tie for his twenty-first birthday, which he tells me you are wearing, is this correct?'

The man indicated it was.

The medium went on, 'There is to be a special memorial service for your son in a church in Shawlands on the south side of Glasgow next month and his brother will stand up and read for him.'

He stopped speaking for a moment and tilted his head up to the left as if trying to hear something in the air around him before continuing.

'He wants Alan to know that he loves him and that he thanks him for what he is doing. Alan is the brother who will speak for him next month, is this correct?'

The couple were holding each other by now and the woman said that everything was correct and she thanked Albert for the message. Then he tilted his head again and went on to his next contact as if nothing special had occurred.

It was the last message of the night when I was picked out of the congregation, and just in the same way as the others before me, I was startled when the small man said, 'You at the back, you know who Stuart is, who is dying of AIDS, is this correct?'

Stuart was a friend of my friend Christine. She had told me about him and asked if I could go to see him in hospital and maybe shave him and cut his hair to tidy his appearance for him. I had only had the conversation with her that afternoon, so when I heard this I was a bit stuck for words. The other thing about this message was that AIDS was still very taboo at that time and even the mention of it made people in the church gasp.

'Yes, I know who this is.' I forced out the words and felt the rest of the room looking at me.

Mr Best proceeded. 'Brian is here. He tells me he died in a fire and that he worked in the theatre, is this correct?'

'Yes.'

'He mentions something about shaving someone – no, wait, are *you* to shave this young man who has AIDS?'

'Yes, that's correct.'

'Brian assures me that this won't happen, as they are all gathered around him now and they will help him over on the last day of the month.'

This was something I couldn't know, so I didn't answer. Instead I let the medium continue.

'I am being told that you are a medium,' he said, then paused and added, 'you look a bit young, though.' He stopped again, looked up to his left, then said, 'You are a medium and you saw this man Brian just after he died, is that correct?'

'Yes, I did.'

'Will you tell Christine that Brian is fine on the other side and thank her for what she is doing for Stuart?'

'Yes, I will.'

'Young man, can you come and speak to me at the end of the evening? I would like to talk to you about your mediumship.'

'Yes. Thank you, Mr Best,' I said as the entire room looked at the person at the back of the hall that Albert Best wanted to talk to about his mediumship.

Brian had worked in a theatre in Glasgow as an electrician. Stuart had been a friend of his as well. He did pass on the last night of the month. I never got to shave him.

I never got to speak to Albert Best at the end of that demonstration either, because so many people were waiting to talk to him, but something told me it would not be the last time we ran into each other.

Testing the Spirits

I had no idea that within one year of watching the great Albert Best that I would be standing on the platforms of Spiritualist churches giving demonstrations of mediumship, and yet you might think that as a budding medium that I would have picked up some knowledge of this, quite apart from all the predictions I'd been given.

I believe that at this time in my life I was still trying to process all the wonderful things that were going on around me. I was developing my gift with Mrs Primrose, reading books about remarkable people with incredible spiritual abilities and often watching and listening to them in the Spiritualist churches around Glasgow. It was quite something for a young man who had been brought up without religion in his life and who had no real concept of God, or what happened after death, if anything.

I write this today with absolute knowledge of the spirit world and certainty of the afterlife, but it took me quite some time to even believe all the stuff that was going on around me. I can tell you with hand on heart that I examined and tested every detail of every message I received from mediums or through my own meditations, and I would ask any who follow in my footsteps to do the same. Don't just accept things for the sake of it. Even if your beliefs lean towards this kind of thinking, always insist on proof from the other side. Don't be afraid to ask spirits to *prove* that they watch over you.

Mrs Primrose often said that to test the spirits was a good thing, but after they had answered you three times, you had to accept what they were telling you. Once could be imagination. Twice might be coincidence, but three times meant that there was definitely something going on.

In the very early days of my mediumship I worked only in Mrs Primrose's church, then after a short while I was asked to work in the churches around Glasgow, and as my reputation spread, I found that I was asked to travel further afield.

I always remembered that my healer John had told me that I would travel around the world as a medium and spiritual teacher and that I would spread the word of spirit to many people, but I still never really saw that happening.

One night I was sitting in the congregation of Mrs Primrose's church when the visiting medium, Mary Armour, who became great friends with me later in life, stood on our little platform and said to me, 'Young man, I have a tall man standing with me who says he is your grandfather and that he was the only one of your grandparents that you met in this life. He mentions the name of "Barney" to me and he talks about the Glasgow shipyards and I feel that he would have worked there during some part of his younger life. He died in his early seventies.'

All of this was true – three of my grandparents had died before I was born, and Barney, who was my mother's father, had come to live with our family before he died at the age of seventy-three, when I was eleven.

Through the medium, my grandfather told me that I would write a book and not to worry because it would take time, several years in fact, but then many more would come. I would tour America and speak before thousands of people each night and my life would change so much within the next three years that I couldn't imagine it.

Now I don't know whether it is the case that by training our mind to think in a certain way, we can shape our future, but I look back at that time in my life, when my future must have been so uncertain, and I believe that I must have had many choices before me. There would have been different future possibilities and maybe I would have had to take the correct action before any of these predictions had a chance of being realised.

All I can say for sure is that a year after this, I was watching another of our very good mediums, a Mrs Clem Harvey of Glasgow, and she said that my grandfather on my mother's side of the family was communicating and wanted me to know that my future was being sorted out and that I would soon be on my way to what I should be doing. She said that he wanted me to know that I had a destiny as a medium and spiritual teacher and that I should get a new passport, as I would need it for all the travel I would have to do. As well as America, he said there were now tours of Australia and South Africa in the pipeline, and when they happened I shouldn't be afraid, but should trust the destiny that the spirit world was mapping out for me.

Mrs Harvey stopped her message for a moment and then said, 'Goodness, you will have an audience of 5,000 people!'

Again, what could I do with this information? I remember talking to Mrs Primrose about these messages and she told me that everything that had been said would come to pass, but after her death, not in her time on Earth.

Believe it or not, soon after Mrs Primrose's passing my life did change dramatically and everything these three mediums had told me came to pass. I did write a book, and though I initially self-published it, it was picked up by a publisher and through them I toured America, where each night 3,000 people filled arenas, and then I went on a tour of Australia, where on one occasion, when I shared the platform with Louise L. Hay, the founder of the publishing company, we spoke in front of 5,000 people. And yes, after that I did a tour of South Africa in the same way.

Another Prophecy Fulfilled

Back in the early 1990s, as I began to gain more of a reputation in the Scottish Spiritualist churches, I was asked to attend some of the bigger events, so when I was asked if I would be one of the mediums demonstrating at the Glasgow Association of Spiritualists for their 125th anniversary with another popular medium, I was honoured to do so. I had no idea that the other medium would be Albert Best. When I found out, I began to feel very nervous indeed.

In the early days of giving demonstrations of mediumship, I, like most mediums, suffered terribly from nerves; I think anyone who has to speak in front of a crowd does. When I walked into the mediums' room at the side of the church that night, I was shaking like a leaf. I wasn't just going to meet that man again, I wasn't just going to speak to him, I was going to have to stand with him on a platform and give proof of life after death.

However, Mr Best, as I called him back then, was nothing but gracious to me that night. He put me at my ease and encouraged me to do my best. I recall that as soon as I began to get my first spirit contact, my nerves disappeared and I was flowing. I told a woman in the front row that her husband had recently passed and that I got the name of Jim and that he had watched her the previous day as she had purchased medicines from a chemist's shop in London Road, all of which she accepted. I then gave the message that Jim was watching over her and wanted her to know that when it was their wedding anniversary in April he would be with her to help her move forward. Details like this may seem mundane, but they can be verified, and something that may seem insignificant can be important proof. Then other evidence and messages came through for other people, and soon I had finished my part of the demonstration.

I will always remember that when Albert got up to speak he told the people that he was very impressed with my mediumship and saw that I had great potential. I felt so relieved to have got it over with and grateful for his comments about what I had done.

Then he gave his opening message, which began, 'The

lady in the blue coat, your son is here. His name is Alan and he was decapitated on a railway line between the towns of Coatbridge and Airdrie in 1979, is this correct?'

Now that is what I call an opener.

Albert gave the woman many words of comfort and went on to give many other similarly detailed messages that night.

At the end of the event I drove him home and we talked for hours, or rather he did and I listened, completely fascinated by his accounts of working with the earlier mediums I so admired, people like Helen Hughes, Nan Mackenzie, the great London medium Joe Benjamin, Stewart Lawson, an amazing medium who worked out in South Africa, and the wonderful Estelle Roberts. He had met and worked with the psychic researcher Arthur Findlay at his home, Stansted Hall, now a training college for mediumship. He even told me of a séance he sat in with the famous Helen Duncan in Glasgow, where animals appeared. These were people's pets, and all of them were identified by their owners. More on some of these mediums later. Some of their work was truly extraordinary.

That night was a real eye-opener for me and it was great to hear Albert's stories from him personally. We remained friends until the end of his life in 1996.

Only a year after our first proper meeting, he was sitting in my living room with some of my friends when my phone rang. It was Christine, saying that she had a strong urge to come and see me and would this be okay?

I didn't mention anything to Albert or the others, but I had a feeling that this might be the moment Mrs Duffy had seen several years before.

Christine knew that I had become friendly with Albert, but she had never met him and her life had changed and she had been very busy with a new baby and some studies she was working on, so there hadn't been a chance for us to arrange a sitting with Albert for her. I had never told him about Mrs Duffy's prediction either, so imagine how we all felt when Christine entered the room and Albert said, 'Smoke, smoke – I smell smoke, and I have to speak to this woman in private.'

The rest of us left the room and when the reading was over, Christine told me that she was completely blown away and that she felt that she had had a conversation with her brother. She said that the love that had come through was so powerful that she was lost for words.

The whole thing had been so spontaneous and Albert had had no idea who Christine was – there hadn't even been time for an introduction – but, just as predicted, the information he gave her meant that she would never doubt that there was life after death again.

'An Unbelievable Truth'

As a medium, I bring through messages to help people understand that not all mediums and psychics are fake, that some have just been born with extraordinary abilities that have shown them that the human spirit is something other than a body with a brain and five senses. I really want to prove to people that there is more to life than meets the eye.

It was for this reason that I was happy to take part in the scientific tests of Professor Archie Roy of Glasgow University some twenty-odd years ago. Archie had become interested in my mediumship after working with Albert Best. It was Albert who had recommended that he speak to me, saying he had faith in my abilities. Also, Archie's associate, Tricia Robertson, had seen me demonstrating my mediumship and thought I would make a good subject for the tests. This was indeed a great honour, especially for such a young medium.

The tests, carried out over five years, were called the Robertson–Roy experiments. The idea was to see if a medium gives purely general information or information with a 'strike rate' greater than chance. Full details of all the experiments in which I and other mediums took part can be found on the internet (*see Further Reading*).

Briefly, the first test was a simple demonstration of mediumship for the public, where scores were counted based on the number of hits we got with the messages.

The next test was a blind test, where we worked for an audience but we couldn't see them and had no idea if they were saying we were correct or not. Only Tricia and Archie knew, as they collected the scores.

Then there was a test where I was in a room in the university with a microphone and a diagram of a room situated somewhere else in the university. I had no idea if there were even people there or not, but I gave twenty statements that related to the seat I chose on the diagram and that was that. There were people in the other room, but no one was told the seat number they were sitting on and all were given score sheets to tick or cross when I made a statement. At the end of this test, only one person in the room could accept a high percentage of the evidence given in my statements, and that was the person sitting in the seat I had chosen.

One of the last tests was conducted in a triple-blind manner where neither I nor the recipient knew it was going to happen and the researchers themselves didn't know the details of the test. I was taken by surprise by Tricia visiting my home one morning, asking me to again choose a seat, only this time in an arena. Once again I did this and gave twenty statements that came to my mind and Tricia sealed them in an envelope and posted it to an address given to her by Professor Roy. The following week Professor Roy arrived at the venue and gave a talk to a large audience. During the talk, he asked them to take part in a test. He read out my statements and asked everyone to consider them and tick any that had meaning for them. Once again the only person who could understand an amazing 98 per cent of what I had said was sitting in the seat I had chosen.

At the end of the tests, I was asked by Tricia if I would give Professor Roy a private sitting in her home. I had grown very fond of the great man and would have done anything he asked. I remember being quite surprised by the request, however, as although he had showed that he was in favour of my work, Archie was always the scientist and would sometimes stay on the fence no matter how many times I provided good evidence in his tests. Even when I scored 98 per cent in the triple-blind test, he just said that it was very interesting. It made me wonder what he could hope to find out from a sitting with spirit.

All I can tell you about what happened next was that I sat in Tricia's front room with him and she took notes and recorded the session on her tape recorder as I spoke. It became one of the rare sittings when I went into a trance and my spirit guide took over. One minute I was speaking in my own voice to Archie and the next I had fallen into a dreamlike state and felt the presence of my guide, and I allowed it to continue.

What happened next was quite extraordinary, but because it was so personal to Archie and his life I wouldn't feel comfortable sharing it in public. The gist of it was that he had a very serious situation going on, which only he and Tricia were aware of, and he wanted to ask a medium he truly trusted to try to get answers for him. I believe that I was taken into a trance so that my mind was toned down and that I could not allow my personal feelings to come into the reading.

All I can say is that at the end of the session Professor Roy was pleased with the outcome. He had not only had his questions answered, but had received information about the next ten years of his life, which was to prove accurate. He was able to complete everything he was told he would do and the strange thing was that he died almost exactly ten years later, though at no time during the message was death predicted.

No matter how many times I was able to give convincing evidence of spirit communication in the many tests I did for him, I believe that personal reading convinced him more than anything else he had experienced. It really doesn't bother me that I cannot write the details of that session in this book, because I know that it meant so much to a great man of science who also became my friend.

It was Archie's last comment that I always remember. Actually, I even used it as a book title. 'What just happened was unbelievable,' he said. 'In fact it was an unbelievable truth.'

What I got from the reading I gave Archie was the understanding that the future isn't set in stone and when we are conscious enough to make definite choices in moments of uncertainty, new timelines can begin. These can be seen clearly by the spirit world, and if it is in our best interests to know the future, they can reveal it to us.

Today is the Birthplace of Tomorrow

'There's life in the air,' I was once told by a wise old man in the spirit world and I know this to be true. Back in 1997, when I was working as a tutor at the Arthur Findlay College in Stansted, I sat with the course organiser, a medium called Don Galloway, and watched him give a message to a young man and woman, maybe in their early thirties, who had come along to his demonstration of mediumship. Picking the woman out from the crowd of more than a hundred people, he told her that her father in the spirit world wanted to pass a message to her. The young woman accepted this, as she had lost her father in recent months. Don went on to give very accurate details of the spirit man's life and death, and then said, 'Your father has just told me that he will be there next June when you are holding a baby boy in your arms and you and the gentleman sitting beside you will have had your dream come true.'

For a moment there was no reply – instead the couple mumbled something to each other. The medium wasn't put off in any way and gave more evidence from other family members before moving on to speak to the next recipient in the audience.

During the week I got to know the woman better, as she was one of the students in my class. She told me that she had had wonderful evidence from Mr Galloway, but that she and her husband had found that they couldn't have children, so with the baby, they were thinking of adopting, and she wondered if that was what he was seeing. I remember telling her that time would tell and that when mediums gave messages of things that hadn't yet happened, it was down to trust.

I knew Don Galloway was a very good medium and a very

responsible one too, so deep inside I felt that what he had been seeing would come to pass, and also that it was their own child he had seen, but it wasn't for me to add anything to another medium's message. I knew that Don was at times a very accurate seer, too, though on this occasion he had said the information was coming through the father of the young woman who was in the spirit world, so he had received it through his mediumship.

The following September I was giving a service in the Spiritualist church in Lincoln when a couple approached me, showing off a baby bundled in blankets. It was the people who had had the message from Don a year before, and yes, it was a boy who had been born in June, and no, he was not adopted, but had been conceived naturally.

How could anyone come up randomly with this type of message to people they haven't met before? It may sound strange to most people, but when you have witnessed as many strange but true spiritual messages and happenings as I have, it starts to sound like the norm! What it enforces for me is that the spirit world knows things about us – past, present and future – and if the conditions and the time are right, they can touch our world with that knowledge.

From all the experience I have had of messages of the future, either hearing about them, giving them or receiving them, I am also convinced that the future isn't certain. I believe that there was an argument in the 1920s between Albert Einstein and Niels Bohr about the future. While Einstein believed that it was certain to a degree, Bohr argued that it was only certain when it could be measured and came into being. In my humble opinion, the future only exists when an action or intention has begun in the here and now, meaning that something that wasn't thought possible one moment can actually happen in another because of the action, or intention to create an action, taken at any given moment. A person who is on a straight path may find that path altering in the blink of an eye because of one simple action, thought or even word.

According to a spirit guide I once heard teaching us, even the spirit world only knows the most probable future. They have more awareness of it than we do, but even so, the future, like the universe, is forever in motion, and change is the only certainty we can depend on.

Having said that, I know for certain that when a person receives a message which causes them to believe that they are governed by a higher force, it can bring peace and healing into their life. This can be incredibly important in difficult times.

5

Support in Troubled Times

Looking back at the birth of Spiritualism to uncover the higher purpose of it all, I would say that the spirit world knew that there were going to be wars and tragedies on scales never seen before and that people would need more than just religious prayers and belief to see them through. Greater proof was needed.

It was also a time in which many people were losing touch with the religions they had been brought up in and looking for their own answers. I believe that the world was waking up and the timing was right to allow people to have personal spiritual experiences – encounters with their loved ones in the hereafter that took their thinking beyond belief and into acceptance of life after death.

Voices in the Dark

One man whose thinking was completely changed by the evidence given by a medium was the very successful businessman Arthur Findlay of Glasgow.

In his book *Looking Back* (Psychic Press, 1955), he tells of walking home on a Sunday evening in 1918 after visiting his wife, who was in a nursing home, and taking a path that would change his outlook on life for ever. Strolling aimlessly along the streets of the city, he came across a sign saying 'Spiritualist Church'. Having no idea that such a denomination existed, he ventured inside to listen to a lecture given from the platform by a very ordinary man, not dressed in priestly robes or collar, but saying some wonderful things about the afterlife which intrigued him.

At the end of the speech, he went up to the man and asked him if he really expected people to believe what he had just said about life after death, and to his surprise the man said that he didn't expect people just to *believe* in what he said, but to look for proof.

This reply appealed to Mr Findlay, as he never just accepted things, especially to do with religion, and had often found himself at odds with his parents over their belief in Christianity and referred to them as gullible or easily led.

The Spiritualist man offered to get him proof of survival if he wished it, saying if they met the following evening he would take him to see a man who could convince him. The offer was too challenging for a mind like Arthur Findlay's to resist and so it was agreed that on the Monday evening he would have his first experience of sitting with a medium.

He was taken to a working-class home where ten people were sitting in a circle. A very humble-looking man called John Sloan was introduced as the medium.

Findlay had taken great care not to give his name to the first man he met, and he didn't mention it to John Sloan either. He sat down as part of the circle, the lights were turned off and the séance began.

In the darkness a man's voice boomed out of thin air and introduced himself to his wife, who was sitting in the circle. The voice gave detail after detail to her and she agreed with everything that was said.

Then another voice came through, a woman's voice this time, talking to someone in the darkened room who said he was her husband. Once again details came through thick and fast, and all were accepted as truths. This was followed by the voice of a child, then that of another man, this time speaking with a different accent. Findlay thought it was so clever the way this little working-class man calling himself a medium was able to create so many voices and convince people that they were their dead relatives.

The séance lasted for more than two hours and Mr Findlay was feeling more impressed by the acting talents of this so-called medium than by anything 'supernatural', when a man's voice boomed out in front of his own face: 'I'm your father, Robert Downie Findlay.'

Now in a state of shock, he was wondering how these people, no matter how clever they were at acting, could access his father's exact name. It wasn't only that, as the voice, which even sounded like his father, began talking to him about an occasion some fourteen years earlier, when he had wanted him to be a partner in his firm but hadn't been able to get the other partner to agree.

This was a very personal episode in Arthur Findlay's life, and was known to only one other person apart from him and his father, and that person was also dead. His name was David Kidston and he had been his father's business partner and later for a period his own business partner. So you might imagine his amazement when the voice of his father then said, 'David Kidston is standing beside me and he would like to talk to you about this matter.'

David Kidston then spoke directly to him and apologised to him for not voting him onto the board when he had been asked.

This was incredible and sent Arthur Findlay's mind into a whirl. This matter was something that had plagued his mind for some years and now he was receiving an apology from the man responsible, only that man was dead.

This first encounter with the spirit world and the mediumship of John Sloan were to open Arthur Findlay's mind to many, many new possibilities. He knew that no one in that room could have known the information with which he had been presented. And how could John Sloan, a humble working-class man who worked long hours, have accessed all the details given in the séance and produced the voices of people's loved ones so accurately?

On leaving Sloan's small home at the end of this bizarre evening, Arthur Findlay asked how much he should pay for the séance and one of the other sitters told him that Mr Sloan never accepted payment for what he saw as a duty to the bereft. This also didn't strike Findlay as the workings of a fraud.

Over the many years that followed, Arthur Findlay tested the mediumship of John Sloan, and these tests are outlined in the many books he wrote on his findings concerning the Glasgow medium. I have read these books and though I do believe that genuine mediums should have no problems in being tested up to a point, I do find it quite extraordinary that Mr Sloan allowed this to happen before, during and after almost every séance he took part in with Arthur Findlay and the many other people who wanted to look into his amazing abilities.

So many fantastic messages are recorded in the books of Arthur Findlay that you would either have to believe he was a complete fool for believing them or that they were some of the most amazing episodes of mediumship ever experienced.

If you read his life story, you will get an insight into how intelligent this man was and also how cautious he was when investigating mediums. I would have to say that he did more for the intellectual promotion of mediumship and Spiritualism than any other person and I truly believe the mediumship of John Sloan to be nothing but honest and authentic.

In one incredible account of Sloan's gift, he was taken by Findlay to London to demonstrate his mediumship for the widowed Queen Alexandra. Among the witnesses to this were Arthur Conan Doyle, Sir William Crookes, Sir Oliver Lodge, Sir Thomas Lipton and an American scientist called Mr Byrd, who during the séance had a friend of his in the spirit world talk to him about an exact conversation they had shared on the Brooklyn Bridge. 'This is all true,' he replied, 'but how can you speak to me when you're dead?'

Many great messages came through in that séance, but Arthur Findlay did not make them public, only saying that the queen was totally satisfied that her late husband, King Edward VII, had definitely communicated with her.

When I read such accounts, as they happened before my time I can only look at the reputation of the witnesses who reported them. Arthur Findlay was a very credible witness, as he made it his task to ensure that no medium he tested, Sloan or otherwise, could have the opportunity to cheat. He would make Sloan hold water in his mouth on occasion to rule out ventriloquism. He would make him work in new and unknown settings so there was no chance of him being able to set anything up in advance. He tested every medium he worked with in one way or another. He would book anonymous readings with mediums and often send other people in his stead, and so on. He always moved the séances to different places and made sure that no one accompanied the medium that could have been in league with them.

I would say that he did his due diligence in testing the mediums, as he wanted mediumship to be reported on scientifically and with a measure of scientific control. He graded the evidence mediums gave A for excellent, B for good and C for obvious statements. He always had his stenographer with him who copied verbatim notes of every séance he took part in. As a result, he was taken very seriously by his peers in psychical research and his books were well received.

After his own death, he left his stately home in Essex, Stansted Hall, to become a college for the study of mediumship and the afterlife; it is known today as the Arthur Findlay College and is a place where upcoming mediums go to develop their gifts.

Mediumship in the Blitz

You only have to look at the level of mediumship during the two major conflicts of the twentieth century to see that as the world approached its darker times, mediumship grew stronger, almost in response to the call of desperate human consciousness. So many mediums worked tirelessly during this very difficult time and I can only imagine how important their work was during the very dark times of the war. But I have heard some first-hand accounts of it.

I had the privilege of meeting an old medium called Ivy Scott when I was working with her in London in 1996. She was ninety-four years old then, and still able to stand on the platform with me, just a nipper aged thirty something, and give great evidence from the other side. I must say it was an honour to stand with this great lady of spirit, but equally amazing was the story she told me after we had both worked.

During the early 1940s reputable mediums like Ivy Scott and Helen Hughes were sought after by many people who had lost loved ones to the war, or who had no idea if their beloved family members and friends were dead or alive. It would be safe to say that good and trusted mediums were highly in demand.

Ivy told me that one night during the Blitz in London she was sitting in the small back room of a neighbour's two-up two-down house, waiting to see a woman who had grave concerns about her two boys, who were fighting in Europe. No word had come back from them in months. She said that she had a strong feeling that both were alive, even before the woman entered the room, but she wanted confirmation from the spirit world before she would say such a thing to the frightened woman, so she tuned in.

She felt the presence of a woman on the other side and knew she would be the spirit who would bring information forward to the enquirer. As the sitter took her place opposite her, she held her hand and began to speak to her to give her comfort and tell her she would do her best to get some information for her.

Then Ivy felt a cloud of darkness surround her, but she wasn't afraid, nor did she feel that it represented death or grim news. She was a true medium who wouldn't be perturbed by such a thing. Instead, she went deeper into the feeling. She saw the darkness lift and two young men huddled together, both in uniforms, one cradling the other, who appeared injured but not dead.

Ivy described this to the sitter, who began to cry, but gave a meek smile of hope as she listened in. Then she spoke to her about the woman whose presence she could sense. She described her as small and stocky, and for a moment she felt she actually became her. She could even tell that the woman spoke with an Irish brogue, even though she wasn't hearing her at this point. The overwhelming feeling was that this spirit woman was watching over both the young men and that she would bring them home.

On hearing this, the woman sitting opposite Ivy raised her shoulders, almost in a show of strength. Then the medium knew who the spirit woman was and said, 'This is your mammy.'

Once this was accepted, Ivy asked the spirit lady to give her further details, which she did. She first gave her name, Molly, and then said that she had died two years earlier of a heart attack. This was correct. She then went on to say that Tommy and John would come home within the year and their mother would have them there at her table. The boys' names were correct too.

Ivy had an overwhelming feeling that these boys were not to die in the war, but she could feel that there was a soldier now standing beside her who had died recently. She felt that there had been an explosion of some kind which had ended his life. He was not one of the woman's sons, but a nephew by the name of George. The sitter again accepted this.

It was more than a year after this sitting that Ivy heard that both young soldiers had made it home safely. Tommy had had a wound to his thigh, but nonetheless had sat at his mother's table again, just as his grandmother had said.

What struck me about this story was Ivy's ability to sense the presence of the spirit, as well as the extraordinary clairaudience and clairvoyance that helped her read the situation accurately and made her brave enough to give a message in such a dire situation, as no true medium would want to promise false hope. It also makes me wonder how Ivy would have gone about the reading if she got a sense of bad news, but I know the spirit world would have orchestrated this reading, and that is why it happened as it did.

This isn't the last you will hear of the amazing Ivy Scott, who lived to the remarkable age of 104 and who I know was still giving spirit messages to people in the retirement home she went to live in at the end of her very special life.

A Spirit Message in Tunisia

I have found that when the atmosphere is torn by fear of impending doom, extraordinary things can occur.

In Rosalind Cattanach's book about Albert Best, *'Best' of Both Worlds*, she mentions that during the Second World War, Albert, then a soldier in the Inniskilling Fusiliers, was shot and left to die during a battle in North Africa. His body was dumped with six corpses and he should have died, but, as Ros tells it, he heard the voice of his grandmother telling him, 'Get up, get up and run, Albert.' Much to the horror of a German soldier nearby, he did just that.

I spoke to Albert about this years later and he told me that he only met his grandmother once when he was a boy, but she told him that she would be with him in Goubellat. Albert had never heard the word before, and didn't understand it until he was told later that that was where he had been wounded – on the plains of Goubellat near the city of Tunis.

I am certain that many young servicemen and women had experiences like this during the war, because of the extreme conditions they lived through.

Conversations beyond the Front Line

In the book *Fifty Years a Medium*, first published in 1959 (updated as *Fifty Years a Medium*, 1969, reissued SDU Publications, 2006), I came across a marvellous account of the exceptional communication given through Estelle Roberts to a group of families who had lost their loved ones during the Second World War.

Mrs Roberts was considered to be one of the greats when it came to mediumship. Though she would often fill the Royal Albert Hall when she gave public demonstrations of mental mediumship during the war years, it was in private séances, when she would go into trance, that her work reached an even higher level of excellence. When she was in a trance, spirits would talk through her in episodes of direct voice mediumship and speak to their relatives in the gathering, either using her voice or speaking completely independently of her.

In this particular séance, which took place in 1944, the first voice to speak identified himself as Clive Wilson and spoke directly to his parents, who were present, and in a very animated way gave them exact details of his life and death, conversing in his own personality and voice as if he was in front of them, and at times answering questions they put to him.

Also present was Air Chief Marshal Lord Dowding, head of Fighter Command in the Battle of Britain. He interrupted proceedings to ask Clive what his strange nickname was.

The reply came from the spirit speaking through the medium: 'Big Feet.'

This was the correct answer.

The voice of a young man calling himself David White spoke next. He had died at the age of twenty-two when the submarine *Olympus* had been lost off the coast of Malta. He spoke first to his mother, who was present, giving her messages of comfort for all his other family members and telling her that his father was with him on the other side. He then mentioned that a friend of one of the other people present at the séance had joined him. He gave the name of A. B. Austin and said he had been killed in Italy.

At this moment Lord Dowding cut in again, saying that he too had been a friend of this man and commenting that he had been a very fine officer. At this point A. B. Austin himself corrected him, saying, 'I am still a very fine officer.'

Someone calling himself Jenkins came next, asking to speak to his dad and telling him to stop fretting about him and stop bothering the Air Ministry by asking for so many details. He explained that it was nobody's fault that the 'old crate' they had been in had fallen to pieces in mid-air. Jenkins also told his father that he knew he had an actual piece of his plane at home. The father corroborated this; it was a piece of the tail. Jenkins's message was that he wasn't dead and he wanted this passed on to his mother to help her not to grieve so much.

The next voice then came through, saying, 'I'm Arthur Heath. I went down in a destroyer off Crete, but I'm fine now. I've been watching over my brother, who is still out in Palestine. He doesn't believe in life after death, but I'm anything but dead, aren't I?'

This remark was aimed at a woman sitting to the right of the medium, who responded, 'Sounds like you haven't changed, son.'

It was the young man's mother.

Another spirit present was Flight Lieutenant Stevens, who told his wife that he was fine and gave her details that satisfied her that it really was him speaking. He also told her that she would be going to Buckingham Palace in a few days, something she had no knowledge of at the time, but this actually did come to pass, as she was called to collect a medal on behalf of her fallen husband days later.

The séance went on with more incredible information being passed directly from the spirits to their living relatives, all in great detail. So much personal information was given, all of which was relevant, questions were asked and answered precisely, and other predictions were made that turned out to be true.

All the time the medium, Estelle Roberts, was in a deep state of trance, which allowed her spirit guide to control what was happening from the spirit world.

There will be more to come from this great exponent of spirit communication later. I know that during and after the war years her work was sought and trusted by many, among them Lord Dowding and other eminent people, none of whom ever considered her anything other than genuine. Often it is thought that only the gullible get spirit messages and believe in life after death, but on the contrary, in the world wars, just as in the early days of Spiritualism, many highly intelligent people received and believed in the messages from the spirit world.

Anyone who might be sceptical about this medium or others who practised at this time should consider the amount of information you would have to gather to keep such a deception going over so many years. Even in today's high-tech world, it would be difficult to gather so many exact details about people and their families – where they lived, how they died and all the little personal stories that would touch hearts and minds. To do this several times might be possible, but tens of thousands of times all over the UK?

And in wartime, when it was difficult to get such information, quite apart from all the other restrictions, it just wouldn't have been possible, even with a team of researchers.

The other thing to consider is that more often than not the medium wouldn't be privy to who was going to attend a séance, and even if they were given names, very often people used false names so as not to be tricked by the medium.

I must add that Estelle Roberts never charged a penny for these sessions, and that also adds to her credibility, as she really had nothing to gain by doing this for strangers.

An Airman Comes Home

Another example of the work of mediums in the Second World War comes from the book *The Mediumship of Helen Hughes*.

Douglas Hogg of Glasgow was a young air force pilot who was killed when his plane was shot down on 3 September 1940, just one year after Britain's declaration of war against Germany. He was all of twenty-three years old and his death left his parents torn apart with grief.

Mr Thomas Hogg, Douglas's father, sought the help of mediums, but after several attempts still felt doubtful about the evidence he had received and it wasn't until a friend suggested that he book a private sitting with Mrs Helen Hughes, who was due to visit the city, that his mind was changed for ever.

He and his two daughters and his son-in-law attended the sitting and were welcomed by Mrs Hughes, who knew nothing of their lives. Within a few moments, though, she announced the spirit presence of a young airman. 'You are his da,' she said, turning to Mr Hogg. Then, she addressed his son-in-law, saying, 'This boy calls you Ian and passes his fingers through your hair as if to push your head back.'

This was striking evidence for the family. Whenever Douglas entered a room in which Ian was sitting, he had a playful and affectionate habit of running his fingers through Ian's curly hair.

Even more convincing evidence was to follow. 'He calls himself Douglas,' said Helen Hughes. Turning to the two girls, she said, 'You are his sisters, Isobel and Mary.'

Helen then became entranced and after a time Douglas himself took control of her and spoke directly to his family. Mr Hogg afterwards said, 'His conversational characteristics, quite apart from information concerning other relatives who had passed on, left no doubt in our minds as to his identity.'

When Mr Hogg suggested that Ian should ask Douglas a question, he chose what he thought would be a difficult one.

'Douglas,' he said, 'can you tell me the name of the plane you flew up from Ipswich for me about a year before the war?'

Back came the answer like a shot. 'You are pulling my leg now. It was the old *Prague*.'

Douglas gave so much comfort to his family, and at a later session, where his mother was present, he brought other airmen with him to pass messages on to their families.

Mrs Hogg wrote that she was uplifted by the conversations with her son and that he was also able to help other mothers like her. She was convinced that his death was not an end, but a temporary separation.

It was very interesting for me to read that in a trance session Helen gave in 1944 her guide said that one day there would be a way to speak to spirits through a machine, only not in her generation. This fascinates me, as it is something I believe might be possible too. As Helen's mediumship was usually accurate, I will wait with interest to see if her guide was correct in this instance and if it happens in my generation.

'We Are Not Dead'

A most wonderful medium who gave counsel and healing to bereft families in Glasgow during the war years was a lady called Ma Wark. I never had the pleasure of meeting her, but she was the teacher of my teacher, Mrs Primrose. She would hold little meetings in her small front room, allowing war widows to come and communicate with the loved ones they had lost at the front.

Mrs Primrose told me how in one of those gatherings Ma Wark went into a trance and allowed her guide to control her, and five young men spoke through her to their wives, mothers and sisters.

The first was a man called Frank, who spoke to his sister, saying, 'Mary, I'm not dead. Tell Ma and Da I'm fine and let them know I've met Billy. He's just arrived here.'

Frank had only been twenty years old when he had been killed. The Billy he mentioned was his uncle, who had dropped dead of a heart attack one week before the séance.

A Mick Gillespie spoke next, telling his wife that he could see his wee lassie, who had been born when he was at the front. He said he would always watch over her and he was glad his wife had named her Elizabeth. All of this information was correct.

Then two brothers spoke. Mrs Primrose told me that there

were times when both voices were speaking at the same time through the voice of the medium and it was quite incredible.

'Ma, we're here, it's Tommy and Jimmy,' Tommy said. 'You'll get our things sent to you soon.'

'Ma, ah like what yeah did wae the photos of us,' Jimmy added. He spoke in a very different way from his brother, which the mother could easily identify, and she understood the information given, as she had put her boys' pictures into frames and placed them on her mantelpiece that morning.

Then a woman's voice spoke in an English accent to one of the sitters, telling her that she was Alice who had died of TB and she was now with her mother in the spirit world. One of the women in the circle had just lost her mother, and Alice was a cousin of hers from London who had died six months earlier.

All of the information given in this short but amazing session was accepted as true and the people present totally believed that they were speaking to the loved ones they had lost – none of them sounding dead, it must be said.

Ma Wark was known during these years by those who had an interest in Spiritualism, but she will never have been heard of elsewhere. Yet she dedicated her life to helping people for no monetary gain, just because she could. Though I cannot personally vouch for her mediumship, my teacher was as honest as the day was long and, believe me, if she even sniffed fraudulence, all I can say is God help the person who tried to dupe her.

I must also say that Mrs Primrose informed me that just as this session of mediumship ended, the house was raided by police, as often happened in those days when mediums would work from home or small rooms in a town, especially if there was any thought of money changing hands and/or information coming out that might affect morale. Helen Hughes, Ivy Scott and Estelle Roberts all mentioned that they had been visited by government officials, who would pop up from time to time to check what kind of information they were giving out.

There were of course many frauds during the war years – people who used tricks to gain the money of the bereaved. As there were so many grieving people at that time, I imagine it would be easy to do. For every genuine medium practising during the war years, I'm sure that there were ten frauds extorting money out of people.

Albert Best told me that in Glasgow some very unscrupulous people would make a fuss in the streets and say that John Sloan was giving a séance and if they paid a shilling they could get access to it. They would lead the gullible into a dark empty room and close the door and make off with the money, leaving them alone in the dark. Anyone who truly knew John Sloan would have known that he never charged a penny for his work as a medium.

One of the most controversial mediums of the early to mid-twentieth century was another Scottish medium, Mrs Helen Duncan.

That Sinking Feeling

Helen Duncan was born in a small village called Callander, on 25 November 1887. There are reports that, like many mediums, she was able to get spirit messages and give predictions about the future during her childhood. But the most prominent feature of her mediumship was that she was said to be able to produce ectoplasm during a séance, from which spirits would manifest physically and speak to their relatives in this world.

During her life Helen travelled around the country demonstrating these physical phenomena and drawing a lot of attention and controversy. Even today she is still the subject of much argument. The question whether she was a great medium or a fraudulent one is still debated, with many varying opinions across a great cross-section of people.

There has been a lot of speculation about one incident in particular. It is reported, with some validation, that in 1941, during a séance in Portsmouth, Mrs Duncan manifested the spirit of a young sailor, who appeared in naval uniform and spoke directly to his mother, who recognised him as her son. During the conversation he explained to her that the Royal Navy ship he had been on, HMS *Barham*, had sunk and he and many others had died.

The sinking of the *Barham* had not yet been announced by the British Admiralty and so the mother wrote to them, asking for confirmation. In fact the sinking of the ship was not announced for several months after the séance, and some believe this was done to mislead the enemy and also to keep up the morale of British servicemen still at war.

There has been a lot of speculation about how Helen obtained the information. Was she told directly by the spirit of the sailor or had she heard of the sinking through sources in Portsmouth? At the time there were rumours of witchcraft and collusion with the enemy.

Whatever the case, Helen's mediumship was already attracting attention from the authorities, and this only added fuel to the fire. Helen became a subject of investigation by the British government and in 1944 one of her séances was raided by the British Admiralty and she was arrested under the Vagrancy Act, which was a sort of catch-all for various offences, and though vagrancy was only a minor charge, she was held in prison until she was eventually tried at the Old Bailey in London later that same year under the Witchcraft Act of 1735.

Now would be a good time to tell you a story I was told by my teacher, Mrs Primrose, about this medium. If you will recall, I told you that my teacher was as honest as the day was long and when it came to mediums she was very observant of their claims, as it meant so much to her to prove that spirit communication was genuine. So allow me to share her account of sitting in a séance with Helen in the late 1930s in a house in Glasgow.

Mrs Primrose told me that she and another woman were asked to perform a body search of Helen before proceedings got underway. The two women watched this rather big lady, a whole 22 stone in weight, strip down to her knickers and then they searched her body and discarded clothes. Once they were satisfied that she was clean, they put a simple black gown over her almost naked body and escorted her to a chair in the corner of the room before drawing a black curtain in front of her. Here the medium could have no contact with anyone, so no one could pass her anything. I must also point out that this small gathering was held in the house of a person whom Helen had never met before and Mrs Primrose and the other searcher sat on either side of the curtain so no one could get near the entranced medium. Every precaution was therefore taken to prevent cheating.

At this point the main light was switched off and replaced by a dim red light from a small lamp beside Mrs Primrose. Shortly after this, a white mist appeared to flow out from under the curtain. Mrs Primrose told me that it was ectoplasm and that it got thicker and grew in an upwards direction until it formed the shape of a tall thin man of around six foot, much taller than Helen, who was five foot nothing and very broad.

The man spoke to the sixteen people gathered there, telling them that his name was Albert and he was Helen's guide and would help to bring through the spirits who wanted to communicate with them.

Then the ectoplasm changed from the form of the Albert character into that of a small girl, who spoke with her mother, and then that of another man, taller in size again, who spoke to his wife. Several more spirits came through and this went on until almost the end of the séance, when a woman claiming to know Mrs Primrose appeared. It was a neighbour she hadn't seen in some time, and she hadn't even known she'd died. The spirit woman told her that she would see her husband the following evening and that she must tell him that she was well in the spirit world, and she must not appear alarmed, as he had had his right leg amputated.

After the séance Mrs Primrose and the other lady helped Mrs Duncan to dress, and as usual the proceedings ended up with cups of tea and conversations, etc. My teacher told me that she was satisfied that Helen had not cheated or had accomplices to aid her. As for her own message, the only thing she could do now was to wait to see whether it would be corroborated.

The next evening Mrs Primrose was at her own church, and at the end of the service she noticed that the husband of the spirit lady was sitting at the back of the congregation. She walked towards him to greet him, and when he tried to stand up, she saw he had indeed lost his right leg. She told the man about the previous evening, passed on his wife's message and told him of her prediction that they would meet that evening.

All in all, she wanted me to know that Helen Duncan might have been controversial, and she couldn't vouch for everything she did as a medium, but on the occasion when she observed her, she had brought through accurate information, including a prediction.

Something for the sceptic to note here is that even if Helen had had the means to dupe everyone there after her search, she would still have had to have had information about Mrs Primrose's old neighbour, including the amputation of her husband's leg, and prior knowledge that this man would turn up out of the blue to Mrs Primrose's church the following evening. I believe that it was because of this message, which was not for her, but to be passed on to someone she didn't know she was to meet, that my teacher gave her approval to the mediumship of Helen Duncan.

Now many will say that Helen's reputation worsened after this and that she operated as a professional medium and therefore cheated people for cash. I would advise those who wish to investigate the work of this medium to read more deeply than just opinions on Wikipedia or sceptical websites.

In 1944, at Helen's trial under the Witchcraft Act, hundreds of people came forward as witnesses to try to help her case, but not all were allowed to testify. It was clear from the outset that she was being treated as a public nuisance, and Winston Churchill called it 'the tomfoolery trial', so when Helen offered to perform a séance for the jury, which she said was her only real way of defending herself, the judge did not entertain the idea. She was convicted and served nine months in Holloway prison for women in London.

We have no way of knowing if mediums in the past such

as Helen Duncan cheated all the time or just occasionally, when they couldn't produce the real thing, or whether they were truly authentic, other than through the testimony of those who witnessed them at work. Witnesses are all we have when we look at the past, and what we are left with is deciding just how credible those witnesses are.

I deliberately used the testimony of Mrs Primrose, for I have never met a more honest woman or one of sounder mind. If a medium was recommended to her church, she would allow them to demonstrate, but if she thought for one second that their work wasn't totally honest, she would stand up during their demonstration and stop them in their tracks. I saw her do it myself. She was someone whose judgement I would trust absolutely. So I can say that whatever the truth about Helen Duncan, she had some extraordinary gifts and used them honestly at least some of the time.

I have found it quite amazing to research the mediumship of the past, particularly the Second World War. I know that there were many people suffering loss at that time and filled with fear, but it astonishes me when I see the great effort of mediums like Ivy Scott and Helen Hughes and all the others who can't be named in this book. What impresses me most is how they were willing to travel around the country and give their time and their gift to many thousands of people without any reward other than gratitude. It saddens me that history won't even record their war effort as something that was valuable; instead their work, when talked about at all, is often sneered at and maybe even dismissed as cheating or preying on the vulnerable. It is sad to think that they gave medals to pigeons for carrying messages, yet no honour was given to true mediums who comforted hundreds of thousands of people with messages from the spirit world during these terrible conflicts.

These wartime mediums were very much Earth angels who brought messages of hope and comfort to people whose lives were broken and torn apart by circumstances beyond their control. I hope that many will have found support and validation for their work from a world higher than the one they knew and lived in.

6

Healing the Homeland

I've talked about how Spiritualism burst into people's consciousness in the 19th century and rose to its height in the Second World War. After the war, the movement still attracted many people. I would assume that mediums were still being called upon to help the grieving in the hangover of the great tragedy that had taken place across the world.

By the 1950s, Spiritualism was becoming much more organised, and in 1952 it became a registered religion by an Act of the British Parliament headed by Winston Churchill. So, just over 100 years after the experiences of the Fox sisters in America, Spiritualism could be practised as a proper religion in Britain.

Followers hoped this meant that people might take the subject more seriously. Even though for many years there had been buildings around the country calling themselves Spiritualist churches, some of the stigma of the occult had been attached to the movement and its 'spooky meetings', as they were often referred to. Now members of the general public found it easier to walk into the churches without ridicule, and the practice of mediumship was allowed to take place there. Mainstream thinking was still cautious of the new religion, and orthodox religions frowned upon it. However, the work done by the pioneers who had championed it had not been in vain.

Voices of Comfort and Hope

It was at this time that my friend Albert Best began to gain attention for his work. Though he had started his development just after the end of the war, now he was commanding large audiences in Spiritualist churches around the United Kingdom and would soon start to travel all over the world impressing people with his gift.

One of the things he became known for more than anything else in his work was helping families who had lost children. This doesn't surprise me at all, as he himself had lost his wife, Rose, and three young children in the war when their home in Belfast had been bombed during a German air-raid. Albert had been informed of this by telegram on his arrival at Southampton docks in 1944. I honestly believe that it was because of the depth of his own sorrow that he could go where many others could not, for he could truly understand what it meant to lose your child.

He told me that one of his early messages had been for a young woman sitting at the back of a packed Spiritualist church in Kilmarnock. He called her by her married name: 'You must be Mrs Clark, is that right?'

The woman confirmed this.

Though Albert had never met her before, he went on, 'You are the mother of Daniel. Your son died in 1949. He was killed on the Kilmarnock road when a car skidded out of control, is that correct?'

'Yes,' she said, 'that is correct.'

Albert continued, 'Mrs, he wants you to know that you have to stop blaming yourself for his death, as you were definitely not to blame. You believe that you should have held his hand tighter, but you could never have known what was round the corner. Your boy tells me that you haven't had a proper night's sleep since he died, and he really doesn't want you to go on like this. Please, don't live the rest of your life with this as the only memory you have of your son. If you can, try to live on and get back some of the love you had when he was with you in this life. Then you will truly feel his presence, though he is in the next life.'

The woman accepted the message, and at the end of the demonstration, Albert invited her to his sanctuary, where he practised spiritual healing. Over a period of about six months she went to him once a week and by the end of her sessions was back living her life. She returned to work and found that she could now try to help her husband deal with his grief too. It was a combination of the message and the healing that gave this lady some comfort after her terrible loss and, I'm sure, help her to carry on.

I would say that it was around this time, during the 1950s and 1960s, that spirit messages began to change. Even though great evidence of life after death was still given by the mediums, there seemed to be more advice coming through from the spirit world to accompany this, and therefore more healing taking place because of the messages.

It is my belief that the main core of mediumship is healing. It may be emotional healing, as in this case, but it can be physical healing too. It is interesting that the birth of modern Spiritualism and the emergence of so many mediums also highlighted the wonderful work of so many spiritual healers.

Spiritual Healers

Healing has been a part of our world as long as we have. Every culture and society down the ages has benefited from incredible people who could heal the sick. Such people were often called shamans or medicine men and women, and worked with invisible powers or 'magical' potions.

With the birth of Spiritualism, many people claiming to be healers found a place they could gravitate to, somewhere that accepted their gift and allowed them to work with it and develop it. I can't tell you how many thousands of people have practised through the years as spiritualist healers, but the number is probably much higher than you think. So many of the great mediums I have mentioned so far were not only able to channel the voices and messages of spirits, but also able to allow themselves to be used as vehicles of healing.

Spiritual healing can be performed in several ways. Some healers simply lay their hands on the patient in the area requiring healing. Others don't touch the body at all, but make passes with their hands around the patient's aura. It isn't necessary for a healer to go into a trance when giving treatment to a patient, though some do, allowing themselves to be overshadowed by a spirit guide or healing spirit, and the personality of the spirit to take control of their movements and sometimes speech, as with trance mediumship, only now with the purpose of advising on the healing.

As you know, I received spiritual healing for six months at the beginning of my spiritual development in order to become a clear vessel for mediumship. I was also taught by Mrs Primrose that before I could be allowed to work as a medium I would have to develop the ability to channel healing from spirit, first to myself and then to others. Her thinking, which came from her own spirit guides, was that if you could develop healing ability, you were naturally going to develop compassion, and that is one of the main elements required to be a good medium.

Love Lifts Us Up

In the course of my work as a medium, I have encountered some truly incredible healers, and I have heard or read about others during my investigations into the subject. My dear friend Albert Best was a renowned healer. I once watched him entering a trance as he healed and a Chinese man speaking through him as his hands simply passed over the person's body. In this case, which was caught on film by a Gibraltar Psychical Research team, a visible lump on a woman's neck disappeared in seconds.

I have already mentioned Albert's healing sanctuary. Over the years he practised there, in Thornhill in Ayrshire, he collected more than 25,000 statements from patients who felt that they had been successfully healed through his gift.

In one of those sessions, Albert and a friend were asked to help a man who looked like an old down and out from the streets. Albert told me that he was brought to him in rags, with a long beard and unkempt straggly hair, and had such a low level of life-force in him that when he lay on the healing bed, to all appearances he could have been dead.

Albert and other healers began to work on him, but at first he showed no response. Nevertheless, they cleaned him up and, to their astonishment, found that he was much younger than they had first thought. In fact, when hair and beard were removed, it became apparent that he was only in his thirties.

He was given more sessions of healing, and then one evening during a trance session a young woman came through from the spirit world claiming to be his wife. She said she had died shortly after they were married and she spoke to her husband in great detail, insisting that he get back into life.

After several more sessions of healing and many discussions with Albert, the 'down and out' left the sanctuary a new man – well, certainly a different man from when he arrived.

Many years later, at the end of a demonstration Albert had given in a Spiritualist church in Glasgow, the man made himself known to him again. Albert was shocked; he truly didn't recognise him. The man explained that when his wife had been taken from him, he'd felt he had nothing to live for. But when she'd spoken to him through Albert, he'd had such a jolt that it had spurred him on to make something of his life for her sake.

Albert couldn't even remember what had been said in the trance session, but the man told him that his wife had said he was to go back to work and save lives. It turned out that he was a doctor, a cancer specialist in fact, but even with all his knowledge he'd been unable to save his wife from the illness, which was why he'd felt particularly defeated. However, after receiving the message and deciding to turn his life around, he'd gone to America, where he had studied further, and he had become one of the top oncologists in his field. I can only imagine that he had indeed helped many people.

When Albert related this account, it made me wonder just how many people out there give up after the loss of a loved one. It was also such a reminder never to judge.

Healing through Messages

I was just twenty-six when I first saw Albert demonstrate mediumship, but I had been sitting in my development group at Mrs Primrose's for four and a half years and learning how to fix my mind to work as a medium in a clear and precise way, just like those who had gone before me. Even people like Helen Hughes, who was a very natural medium, still had to go through a stage of mental discipline to perfect the craft and gain the confidence to take it to larger audiences and deal with the people who would ask questions about it. I was doing the same in my group.

The healing sessions I had received from John were a gift from the spirits who worked with him to help me to lift the frequency of my mediumship to a higher level. As I said earlier, I didn't know this at the time. But watching the mediums in Mrs Primrose's little church in Glasgow helped me to understand the purpose of the work, which is to help people and to show them that their consciousness never dies and that those we think we have lost can still be with us if the conditions allow. Each week a different medium would stand on the small platform and deliver messages to the public. It was the late 1980s and the quality of the mediums who worked there was quite something.

One night a medium called Jane MacKay, a small woman in her fifties I suppose, who was always beautifully dressed and had well-groomed blonde hair, singled out my friend Effie, who was sitting beside me, for a message.

She said, 'I would like to speak to you about a man called Charlie in the spirit world. He was older than you by maybe ten years and for the last two years of his life he became very infirm. You gave him so much of your time that he wishes to come and thank you.'

Effie told her this was true, but didn't venture any more information.

The medium then went on to say, 'He was your husband and he loved you very much and hopes that he was not too much of a burden to you. He also says that James will be fine, even though he has come through quite a time of it with his health, and will you pass on his love to Joe and the other James too.'

That was it, but Effie accepted everything. Her grandson James, who had leukaemia, had come through some very trying times, but was on the mend, and the last part of the message was just a mention to her sons Joe and James, the boy's father. The message was short, accurate and to the point, and carried a very special message for my friend about her grandson, whom she had been very worried about.

The other thing to note here is that the medium named the spirit communicator, Effie's husband, correctly and also accurately described the age difference between them and how his illness had affected him. Mrs MacKay never guessed at any of these things; instead she spoke spontaneously with complete certainty and trust in her gift. I can confirm that she had no prior knowledge of Effie or her life.

Messages such as this often came through on a Tuesday night in our little church and many people benefited from them. It always reminds me what mediumship is about when I remember mediums like Jane. She always gave such a lot of healing in her messages.

Faith Healing?

A small group assembled one evening at the end of our meditation session and asked our teacher how she came to be a medium. Mrs Primrose never really chose to share much about her young days in Spiritualism with us. She was quite a private woman when it came to her own life, but that night she told us a story about how her daughter had been healed by two total strangers and she herself had been guided to follow her destiny.

She had been quite a young woman at the time, married with a baby, and she had realised that the baby, Betty, had developed an illness which had caused her legs to be damaged. Fearing that the child might never walk in her life, she was feeling very low and in her prayers she asked for healing for her child.

Mrs Primrose had a great faith throughout her life, so when a neighbour told her that she knew of people who were healers and might be able to help, she believed that her prayers were being answered.

Her husband, Robert, pooh-poohed the idea. He thought it a waste of time, but this didn't deter her. She let her neighbour take her to a house in Glasgow where a man and his wife examined the baby like physicians and then fetched a basin of lukewarm water and sat the baby in it before making passes with their hands over her small body. Mrs Primrose said they both appeared to be in some sort of trance or other, but there was a serenity to the whole procedure.

When they had finished, they advised her to take the baby home and bathe her legs in salt water and bind them, and that would be it.

Even with the greatest of faith, Mrs Primrose had expected a bit more than this, but later that evening she got it.

Having done what she had been asked to do, she put Betty down for the night and got on with her own chores around the house. When she was standing at the kitchen sink, she told us that she distinctly heard a woman's voice beside her head saying, 'As long as you serve spirit, your child will never have a problem with her legs again.' Not only did she hear the words, she said, but they went through her body as if she had been shot through with some power or force. She told us she could still feel it as she recalled what had happened all those years before.

That took place around 1930 or 1931, and Betty is still, as her sister May explained to me in a recent phone call, running around in her eighties.

Mrs Primrose served the spirit world from the moment she heard the message and was touched by what she called 'the voice of spirit'. Her own mediumistic abilities were awakened at that point, and she developed them and then opened a church to help others to be healed in body, mind and spirit for all the years of her life to follow. I can only assume that even now, in the spirit world herself, she is still serving, due in part to the amazing condition of her daughter's health.

I remember her telling me that there is never a moment when spirits aren't ready to guide us and that all we have to do is trust them. Since then I have tried to do just that, and no matter how difficult this life gets at times, I will never stop trying or trusting. As far as I am concerned, as we walk through this life, no matter how dark or lonely it may become, we are never alone.

The Sleeping Doctor

Mrs Nan Mackenzie was one of the most amazing mediums/ healers to grace the Spiritualist movement. She was born in Yorkshire in 1882 and became a registered nurse in 1906. A year later she married John, a Londoner who had an interest in Spiritualism which he shared with his new wife. She began to develop her own gifts in a Spiritualist circle with him.

Healing seemed to be her natural spiritual gift, but she achieved great results as a medium also and, like Helen Hughes and Estelle Roberts, filled halls during the Second World War, giving thousands of messages to those in desperate need.

As her abilities and her reputation grew, it became clear that she had an aptitude for trance mediumship, which allowed her spirit guide, a Native American, to speak through her, and with this came amazing medical knowledge that allowed her to correctly diagnose illness and effect healing in ways that often shocked the medical profession.

Nan was very rare in that during the trance her guide would diagnose illness and give advice to the patient. This would be forbidden under today's healing laws, but more often than not she was correct, and she never deflected people away from orthodox medicine – in fact she would often refer patients to certain medical practices – so she was quite complementary in her approach.

She herself was consulted by many doctors, including a Harley Street specialist, an eminent psychiatrist and the governor of a London hospital, all wanting to discuss their patients, and she achieved healing results that they regarded as inexplicable.

The author Edward Lanchbery wrote a series of articles

for the paper *ANSWERS* and the following is an extract
from the one dated July 1952:

> *He was an elderly man in intense pain. At the hospital
> he was X-rayed and the photograph showed a large
> stone in his bladder. They would operate, he was told,
> but he would have to wait at least three months until
> a bed was available. Naturally a nervous man, the
> worry and fear of the operation, combined with the
> recurring spasms of acute pain, almost drove him
> distraught. When a friend suggested he should see Mrs
> Nan Mackenzie, a healing medium who practised at
> the M.S.A. (Marylebone Spiritualist Association) in
> London, he agreed; he was in such a state that he said
> he would have tried anything once.*
>
> *Mrs Mackenzie went into a sort of sleep, or trance,
> which lasted for two hours. During this time she has
> practically no consciousness of what is taking place,
> and after the session she is unable to recognise patients
> whom she has been the instrument of treating. Whilst
> Nan is in the trance, a stenographer records every-
> thing she says and does. In this particular case of
> the man with the stone in his bladder, she advised
> him to have another X-ray taken at his hospital
> and reassured him that an operation was no longer
> needed.*
>
> *When he attended his hospital he did ask for another
> X-ray [but] the surgeon told him that was not neces-
> sary as the plate already showed the stone plainly, and
> gave him all the information required for the operation.
> So insistent was the patient, however, that a further
> X-ray was finally taken. The new photograph showed*

no stone in the bladder. An operation was no longer
necessary. He was cured.

The life of Nan Mackenzie was full of stories like this. Some of what she did is recorded in a book written by Rosalind Cattanach, simply titled *Nan Mackenzie: Healer and Medium*. She continued practising healing until she died at the incredible age of 104 in 1986. She healed so many from her sleeping trance state and gave hope in abundance through her exceptional gift of mediumship when needed.

I never met Mrs Mackenzie, but I have worked at the church where she gave so much of her time and healing to people, and many of those who were treated by her told me that you felt better just by being in her company.

One man told me that in the 1970s he travelled from Hong Kong to be treated by this special lady after being told by his doctors that there was no hope for his cancer as it had spread to so many parts of his body. During several treatments with the trance healer, her guide told him that he should still attend a hospital in London, as he would soon be offered a new drug and his condition would then gradually improve. The remarkable thing was, none of this could have been known by him or by the medium at the time of the message, but shortly afterwards he was offered experimental treatment which saved his life. Though the message was true, he explained to me, it was the healing from Nan that kept him alive until he received the medical treatment. He is still fit and active today.

I think that anyone can see that when extraordinary spiritual healers like Nan Mackenzie used their gifts to make people better, one way or another something special could occur. If the new breed of mediums and healers wish to emulate those who went before them, they need only look at the driving force that fuelled these people, and that was true compassion.

The Spirit World Saves a Man's Life

This account, shared with me by medium and healer Brian Robertson, a minister of the Spiritualist National Union who runs a Spiritualist church in Vancouver, Canada, shows that the spirit world tries to help us if there is a chance to save us or to guide us towards better outcomes in our lives. He writes:

> *I was working as one of the demonstrators with the wonderful medium Mary Duffy when I had the overwhelming feeling to speak to a lady in the centre of the room.*
>
> *I began to describe a gentleman from the spirit world, beginning the communication with dates and times, which she said she did not know.*
>
> *I carried on the description, detailing the type of work he did, specifically as a grain farmer. The name of Stanley was important, along with the name of a wife, Rose, with a husband, James.*
>
> *The woman still could not understand, but I felt very strongly that the man was talking about a heart problem within the family that had to be attended to immediately.*
>
> *Once again, she said she did not understand it, and this time I asked if anyone else in the audience was able to take the information. No one responded.*
>
> *Returning to the recipient, the last piece I decided to*

say was that the man communicating was a grain farmer and that he had lived in Saskatchewan. She then responded, saying the only person she knew with a connection there was her husband, but he wouldn't come to anything like this as he thought it was all 'garbage'!

I left the contact at that and carried on with the rest of the demonstration.

Two weeks later, she contacted me to say she had gone home and decided to tell her husband. He knew all the dates and times. Rose was his great grandmother and James his great grandfather. The communicator was his grandfather, Stanley, who was a wheat farmer from Saskatchewan.

On hearing this, he decided to see his doctor. He found himself in the hospital three days later receiving open-heart surgery for a dangerous arterial blockage.

His wife just wanted to share her gratitude. Not only was the surgery successful in saving her husband's life, but it also changed his perception of his life and family.

This is a great example of how the spirit world works. Though spirits cannot save everyone from everything, as I mentioned earlier concerning the timelines our lives run on, if there is a chance to change something for the better, they will take it if the conditions are right to do so.

So many people want to look at physical phenomena when it comes to mediumship and often forget the true essence of what is happening, which is the expression of love. I have often been allowed to feel the love of a spirit person for a family member, and this is something which cannot be recorded or measured, but can be incredibly healing.

7

Love Can Heal the Soul

Brian Robertson just mentioned working with Mary Duffy and I would like to share one of the messages I witnessed from her when we took part in a public demonstration of mediumship in Edinburgh in 1999.

I had just finished working and taken my seat on the stage we were sharing when Mrs Duffy stood up and walked to the far right of the stage, where she pointed to a man I could barely see from where I was sitting.

'Sir,' she said, 'your wife is in the spirit world and she wants you to know that she is so glad you came here tonight because you actually turned back and headed home, did you not?'

'Yes, I did.'

Mrs Duffy continued in her usual polite manner, describing for the man how his wife had died and then naming the cemetery where her ashes were buried. Once again he confirmed everything she said. It was the next piece of information that almost shocked him out of his seat.

'Sir, your good lady wants you to know that she not only witnessed your actions this evening, but she saw you at 2 o'clock this morning when you were sitting on the floor in front of your television, watching your wedding video, which made you cry, and she knows how bad you were feeling at that moment.'

Now, this is something that either happened or it didn't. In this case, the man confirmed what the medium had just stated, and tears ran down his face.

Mrs Duffy went on to produce a message from his wife, who wanted to tell him that it was okay to cry and feel sad, but he wasn't to allow himself to drop to the levels of dark thinking he had experienced in the early hours of that morning. As further evidence, the medium described the room in which he had been sitting in great detail, even down to the colour and pattern of the wallpaper, which his wife told her she had chosen several years before.

All of the evidence was accepted by the man, who started smiling as the medium took him for a walk down memory lane with his wife.

This was a great message, because there was a lot of evidence and the wife in the spirit world was letting her husband know that she could see him and was supporting him, and that was a great comfort to him.

As a medium, I have no doubt that there are times when our loved ones can see or at least sense us from the other side, as this man's wife did. By this I mean that at very poignant moments in our grief, they are able to draw close to us and, with the help of a medium, can describe the scenes they have seen, and sometimes our feelings and so on. In one of the earlier messages by Helen Hughes, for example, a daughter describes seeing her mother standing at her grave in a cemetery. Over the years of my mediumship I have passed on thousands of messages like this to people and noticed how the very essence of such a message can give hope and in many cases open the mind of the grieving person to a new way of thinking.

On this occasion I remember that Mary Duffy told the

man that mediumship cannot totally dispel grief, but it can be a coping device which we can use whenever we feel low in the days and weeks following a loss. I could imagine that when this man's feelings began to take him to a low place again, the thought that his wife was close by would encourage him to look up and fight back against one of the most difficult battles that all of us who live long enough will have to experience.

It has long been my opinion that where there has been a recent loss and there is a very deep sense of grief and a need to make contact with a departed loved one, the intensity of the emotion can fuel the sitting and make it easier for the medium to make contact.

I recall Professor Roy once asking me to give a private session to a scientist he brought to me out of the blue. His idea was that I would have no prior knowledge of his situation and this might be good proof for his colleague. I started the reading and, after twenty seconds of trying, I told the man, who was of course a complete stranger to me, that he hadn't had a loss in his life for more than twenty years and that all I was picking up was the image of a young man playing cricket and laughing. I then got this man's name, but said, 'Sorry, there is no message here. I'm really not getting a strong connection.'

This short session made both men look at the life situations of the subjects they would later bring to the tests that were carried out with me. They noted that when there were still strong emotions attached to a loss, the mediums they tested got stronger information and better evidence in the readings.

This adds more weight to the premise that during times of national crisis, for example wars, when millions of people are dying and fear is at an extremely high level, the power of mediums is much stronger.

There are so many things that I believe can be investigated and studied when it comes to mediumship, above and beyond whether it is genuine or not. I would have thought that with so many prominent scientists having looked into the workings of mediums over so many years, someone would have taken things further. However, it seems we are still, as a society, voicing opinions on the subject rather than looking at scientific facts.

This seems a shame when even Church of Scotland ministers who have researched the topic have been convinced of the truth and importance of spirit communication.

Call Waiting

In 1973 a book called *A Venture into Immortality* was published. The author was the Reverend David Kennedy, a Church of Scotland minister, and the book covered his own investigations into the afterlife following the death of his beloved wife, Ann. He talked about the many encounters he had with mediums, but on meeting Albert Best he was totally convinced that Ann's spirit or consciousness was able to pass information to him from the other side. The book is filled with his research, but for now I will share just a glimpse of what Albert and other reputable mediums were able to do for him, especially regarding how spirits can see us at times.

Ann Kennedy had been dead for three months or so when, during a phone call between the Reverend and Albert, Albert interrupted their conversation to say, 'Your wife is here. She tells me that you are looking for proof of things that you cannot have known about her life, is this correct?'

'Quite correct, Albert,' the minister replied.

'She says that when you talk to her family, you will find a funny story about ballet shoes,' Albert said. 'It is something you never knew about from her life.'

Then he carried on with the normal telephone conversation as if nothing has happened.

To Reverend Kennedy this information meant absolutely nothing until it could be confirmed, but only twenty minutes later his wife's sister called him out of the blue and told him that she just had an urge to speak to him. They hadn't spoken for several weeks before this. So here was his opportunity to ask if she knew of a story about Ann concerning ballet shoes.

To his astonishment, his sister-in-law laughed and said she couldn't believe that he knew about that because it was very embarrassing for Ann. She had walked in on her many years ago and found her trying on her ballet shoes and prancing around the living room on her own, never expecting to be caught.

Reverend Kennedy was taken aback, because this was a definite response to his question to the spirit of his wife, and it had come via Albert, and it was something neither he nor Albert had known about. His explanation of this type of message was that it could not be a form of telepathy and was evidence of the survival of consciousness.

The story doesn't end there, as a short time after the end of the phone call with his wife's sister, the Reverend's phone rang again. It was Albert himself this time, who said, 'I've just had Ann with me again and she told me you had a phone call and she was the one who impressed the caller to call you, though she never said who the caller was.'

This really impressed the minister, as a whole series of events had now taken place which had brought him the answer to a question he had asked of his wife, a question no one else had been privy to, and he had received his validation within a very short space of time. It was his belief that Ann could see all the events from where she was and had obviously, just as she claimed, had a hand in them.

It is messages like this that confirm to me that the spirits of our loved ones watch over us and, if they can, try to let us know of their presence. Reverend Kennedy was trying to test the spirits and investigate the skills of certain mediums at the time, but during the course of his research, he became more moved by the fact that the messages from his wife contained just as much information about his current life as about episodes from her past, making the information much more credible and relevant.

Another story from that book involves a medium called Mrs Findlater, who actually called the minister's home one Sunday evening because she had had a visit from his wife in the spirit world.

Reverend Kennedy had been feeling very tired after his morning service one Sunday and had decided to stretch out on his sofa before preparing for the evening service, which was due to start at 6.30. Such was his feeling of exhaustion that he entered into a much deeper sleep than intended and was only stirred by the sound of ringing in the distance. It was the telephone. He rose to answer it and was surprised to hear the voice of a woman explaining that she was a medium called Mrs Findlater and she had just had to go through directory enquiries to get his telephone number, because his wife, Ann, wanted to tell him to get up now, use his old notes in the drawer and just go.

Mrs Findlater lived miles away from the minister and was acting purely out of trust in her connection to the spirit. How could she have known that when the call was made the minister was asleep and would probably have slept right through the time of his evening service? How could she have known that he had not prepared a service for that night? How could she have known that he had old notes in a drawer, which were always kept there for emergencies such as this?

In his explanation of this incident, Reverend Kennedy mentioned that he would usually rest between services on a Sunday, knowing that Ann would always wake him on time and have everything prepared for him, so it made some kind of sense to him that when he was oversleeping she would find a sensitive to help her. And that, no matter how far-fetched, it does seem to be exactly what happened.

Albert Best shared all these accounts with me personally, but reading Reverend Kennedy's book tells me that he wasn't someone who took every message from the spirit world as law, though. He and his wife had been investigating the survival of the spirit for many years before her passing and he approached the subject with the same caution and common sense that any true psychical researcher would. *A Venture into Immortality* is a very good look into mediumship and life after death, and all the more so because the researcher points out how trivial many of the messages he had were and that some of the mediums gave what he thought could be guesses or general statements that would apply to most people.

The way I look at it is that many people claim to be mediums and psychics, but few can give the type of evidence of those I have chosen for this book. To me, there has to be an element of proof regarding the spirit who claims to be communicating and there also has to be a purpose to the message itself. Without these elements, anybody could give general information and claim it is coming from the spirit world. Many people do similar things when they lose a loved one, for example, like place a flower or a picture in their coffin. If this type of thing is given as evidence, then it had better have some importance to the recipient, otherwise it is just general information or guesswork. If it is backed up with the reason for doing it, on the other hand, it will have more merit and add to the evidence of spirit communication.

Football Crazy

Whilst working for the Spiritualist Association of Great Britain one December with a fellow medium Billy Cook, I became aware of two people sitting in the audience, a man and a woman who looked as though they really needed a message. I could feel my heart go out to them, even though it was Billy's turn to demonstrate first. There must have been some telepathy between us, though, because he ended the message he was giving at the time and told the crowd that a young man had just appeared to him and wanted to speak to his mum and dad. He pointed to the couple I was looking at, though he could have had no idea that I had been drawn to them, as he was standing in front of me. I sent him all the good vibes I could, because I knew in my heart that this was important.

Billy told the couple that their son had died in a crash involving a white van. This was accepted and Billy continued, 'Your son tells me that there are others in the audience from your family. They are sitting on the other side of the room.'

A man sitting on the opposite side from the parents put

his hand up in acknowledgement. He was the brother of the young man.

'He wants you to know,' Billy said, 'that he saw what you did for him for his funeral and it made him very happy.' There was a hush in the room as he paused, then added, 'Well, it's not my team, but he is showing me that you dressed him in a Queens Park Rangers strip.'

There was a gasp around the room as this was confirmed by both parents and the brother laughing out loud and crying at the same time. The audience could feel the value of the message that was coming through and the very positive effect it was having on the family, who, it turned out, were all big supporters of that football team. How amazing that this was something the young man chose to bring back as evidence.

I remember thinking how wonderful it was that Billy had lifted them up and given them a message about something that was important to all of them. It isn't everyone who puts their son in a particular football strip, or any other significant outfit, and here the medium wasn't guessing but was making a very definite statement about what he was being shown by the spirit person. Not only was it correct, but it was helpful and healing to the family because they felt that their son had somehow seen what they had done and wanted them to know he was happy about it. Many families at terrible times like this wonder if what they are doing for the deceased is the right thing or if it would have pleased them, and in this case they got their answer.

The other thing to note here is that the young man in the spirit world could see that there was someone in the family sitting in another part of the room, which contained over a hundred people tightly packed in, making it difficult to distinguish one person from another.

Moreover, I can say for sure that the medium had no prior

contact with this family, as they spoke to us both at the end of our demonstrations and thanked Billy profusely in a way which showed me they had never met him before. I am mentioning this because there are mediums out there who talk to people they know in public demonstrations without acknowledging them as friends or family, but on this occasion that wasn't the case.

'There but for the Grace of God Go I'

So often a spirit message can be the door that opens to a path of healing for the bereft. This was shown in another example from the mediumship of Estelle Roberts in *Fifty Years a Medium*.

At the very end of a public demonstration at the Queen's Hall in London in front of hundreds of people, she was guided to speak to a small, rather dowdy-looking man at the very back of the hall. She asked if she could speak to him in private at the end of proceedings and asked that he be brought to the small room laid aside for her.

As the man entered the room, where Estelle was standing with the journalist Hannen Swaffer, she turned to him and told him to give her the bottle he was carrying in his coat pocket.

The little man appeared shocked, but Estelle insisted he do it. She had been told by her guide that he was carrying a bottle of poison with the intention of ending his life that night and she must stop this.

It was true. The man confessed that several months before he had returned home to find his wife dead on the floor after taking an overdose of pills, and after that he had just given up and had been sleeping rough.

The remarkable thing here is that seconds after hearing his story, Estelle Roberts went into a trance and allowed the wife to come through to speak to him, accompanied by their children, who had also died tragically, and a healing message was given to him, telling him to continue with his life.

Both Estelle and the journalist made it their goal to assist the man. They helped him to find employment and a place to live and within a short time he was functioning in life again.

This account touches my own heart, because when I was a barber I would often go to the down and out centre in Glasgow to cut the hair of men like this. I learned that most of them had given up when they had lost a loved one, and I always thought how sad it was to see the human spirit being broken like this by death. Some of the men came from good backgrounds and had known love and happiness at some point. 'There but for the grace of God go I,' I would always remind myself.

Truly Free and Alive

I have already mentioned the brilliance of the mediumship of Helen Hughes and would like to point out that during the 1940s she travelled the length and breadth of the UK giving demonstrations to halls that were packed to the gunnels. Sometimes as many as 2,000 people would fit into a hall just to watch this amazing woman give exact details and messages from the other side.

A man to whom she gave a message in 1937, six months after the death of his wife, was so taken with her evidence that he wrote an account of it, again quoted in *The Mediumship of Helen Hughes*:

I did not know this lady and she certainly did not know me, or any of my connections or my family at the time of meeting her.

As the sitting began she closed her eyes and seemed to go into a trance and a voice different from her own began to speak to me. The first words spoken were 'Your wife has come. She says she is Jean Anderson Blackburn.' She then told me that I had put flowers of three different colours on top of her coffin, which I had. They were primulas I had taken from my greenhouse that morning. She then told me that my wife wanted me to look at the day of her death as a new birthday, as she was truly free and alive and not dead. She told me that I had some pictures in my pocket and asked me to put them in front of her, which I did. With her eyes still closed, she seemed to be examining the pictures and was able to name everyone in them correctly, even a picture of my favourite dog, who was called Duke.

She then spoke as my wife, telling me that we had forty-two years of real honeymoon. We were married for exactly forty-two years when she died. She named her sister Bella and so many others correctly that were important to our life and in all the names and details there were no errors at all. There were times when I truly felt that I was speaking to my wife Jean.

It is this kind of message that assures me that we cannot die for the life of us. There is no fishing for information, instead exact names, relevant to the recipient, come through without effort. The message itself is full of hope and happiness, which leaves the man with only one conclusion, which is that his wife is still conscious somewhere, even though out of his perception for now, but somehow contactable. I don't believe anyone would doubt there is life after death after such an amazing session and, more than that, it would appear to have cast light into the shadows of his grief. I hope it also shows how amazing this medium's ability was, far beyond the norm.

High Spirits

The older generations of mediums, like Estelle Roberts, Helen Hughes, Ivy Northage and Albert Best, were constantly plagued by people to use their gift and it was quite normal for them to give messages in social situations. They had a sense of duty, a feeling that if they had a spirit there, they should allow them to come through. They were always on call, as it were.

Today things are a bit different and mediums tend not to do that. Part of the development that is taught today is how to switch off to spirit during social situations. We now have a code of ethics that tells us not to freelance our gifts. I was taught to open up when I was meant to and keep closed when I was in everyday situations. I worked for over twenty years as a hairdresser and in all those years of being up close to people who had often had a loss, only once did I give a message. On odd occasions I would get a feeling, but my training taught me to listen and advise people how to go about getting a message rather than give one myself. And I do believe that my mediumship is for those who ask for it and not to just be given out.

This being said, all mediums will tell you they have at least once felt impelled to give a message when not working as a medium. It just happens sometimes. But in my life I have only given messages to people who didn't ask on a few occasions, so few that I can remember each one.

I think that one of my favourite memories of when a message came through unexpectedly was when I was on a jet airliner and gave a message to the pilot while he was flying the plane! I had just finished making a pilot episode for a proposed television show in Teddington studios in London with the TV actress Claire Sweeney, who was to host the programme. At the end of filming she asked me if I was going back to Glasgow, as she was travelling there that night by a private jet provided by her record company. I had never been on a private jet, so the offer was far too tempting to refuse. For a guy who had been brought up in the Gorbals in Glasgow and spent most of his life cutting hair for a living, it was an incredible experience.

I remember how surreal it felt stepping into a small but luxurious aeroplane with padded leather armchairs. I'd never had those in economy class! It was also unfamiliar to be offered drinks before we even took off, but somehow in the midst of my excitement I managed to relax and enjoy the experience. Claire and I began to chat about the day's filming as the plane lifted us into the night sky and before long we could have been on any plane as conversation took over.

It was halfway through the flight when the co-pilot came out of the cockpit and asked if we would like to go up front and experience what it was like to fly a plane. Claire was happy to stay where she was, but I couldn't resist, so up I went and sat beside the pilot, a very good-looking man in his forties, and put on my headphones so that I could hear him above the noise.

As he guided me through the controls of the plane, I got

the overwhelming feeling that a woman was standing next to me. Obviously there was no one physically there, but her presence was so strong that I began to lose the thread of the pilot's conversation, and then I heard her voice in my head saying, 'I'm Margaret.' She continued talking, telling me that she had died of breast cancer and that I should tell her son she was there. Now, this was the very last experience I expected to have on my first ever trip on a Learjet, but I couldn't deny that it was happening.

I started wondering how to tell the pilot, because, as I mentioned earlier, I honestly don't like to just give messages to people who don't ask for them.

Fortunately, he asked me if I worked in the music business, as the plane had been rented by a music company for Claire. This was my opportunity to tell him that I was a medium and watch for his reaction.

I remember to this day how he turned to look at me in a way that told me he was interested in what I had said. It became clear to me that he wanted me to say more about it, so I explained what I did. He said this fascinated him and he'd actually thought about seeing a medium recently.

Without further ado, I revealed what I was experiencing and, with that, the message came through that he was desperate to hear. As each piece of information came, he became very moved. Tears began to run down his face as he shook his head gently from side to side as if in complete disbelief. Margaret had only been dead for six months or so and his grief was very raw, but in his tears I could feel a letting go. It was as if he was releasing months of emotional pain as question after question was answered by his mother in an unseen world.

I have to add that I did have a moment when I wondered

about the flying of the plane, but the pilot was finally able to gather his composure. He thanked me for what had just happened and said that he had had no real idea about how to go about looking for a medium and the fact that he had met one out of the blue made the whole thing more acceptable.

Here again, the messages that came through were much more important than anything else. The evidence of the mother's name and how she died were just to prove her identity. The pilot was carrying so much regret and, without revealing all the personal information, I can say that his mother's message was aimed right at his deepest pain, and the answers she passed to him were focused on healing his inner self.

I know I will probably never meet that man again, but I honestly hope that what happened that night was the start of a healing process that would let him move on with his life in the knowledge that his beloved mother was still a part of it and wanted him to be happy.

Once again, this also showed me that my own mediumship had to have purpose or it was no more than a clever trick.

Soothing the Soul

Coming back down to earth now, I recently worked with a good friend and colleague called Janet Parker. Janet is a Spiritualist minister and is very well respected in the religion. It was when we were both demonstrating mediumship at a small event in northern England that I saw how her gift worked to help heal people on a soul level.

Like many good mediums, Janet singled out a woman in

the audience. She told her that she heard the name 'Barbara', and then said, 'This is your own name, isn't it?'

The woman agreed.

The medium said, 'You have lost your mother in the last year and she's telling me she's called Mary.'

This again was true.

Janet was then able to describe to Barbara how she was feeling at the end of her mother's life, highlighting the sense of regret and helplessness she had experienced. She was able to go right through her life in the last six months, though Barbara was a complete stranger to her. Each episode of grief and depression she had experienced was covered in great detail, until it was revealed that all the thoughts and feelings she was experiencing were unnecessary, as her mother in the spirit world was out of all suffering and was now in a much better state of mind than her daughter could imagine.

As I listened to my friend work with this lady in the audience, I could feel the penny drop as Janet pointed out that Barbara's painful emotions were only affecting herself and that her mother wanted to help her be free of them. She was able to make it very clear that Barbara needed to look at the love there had been between her and her mother and that she had to remember all the good things she had done for her.

After the loss of a loved one, people so often accuse themselves of not doing enough or not changing things that they believe might have made a difference in some way, but such thinking can crush the soul and prolong the grief. Grief can become multi-layered when what begins as a natural feeling of loss slowly turns into self-deprecation and regret.

As I mentioned earlier, I have noticed that so many of our messages now are aimed at helping to lift the mind of the bereft. We still prove that we are getting messages from the spirit world, but the real purpose of our mediumship is to try and help the people who have come looking for answers when they have been left in that terrible sense of disconnection brought by loss. Evidence is given, but the emphasis is on helping people in this life.

Usually the medium doesn't know the dear departed of course, but this isn't always the case.

'I Didn't Know You Were Dead'

Just over two years ago I was giving a demonstration of mediumship in the Arthur Conan Doyle Centre in Edinburgh to a packed crowd when into my mind came a woman's voice – a very strong woman's voice in fact. The strange thing was I recognised her, yet I wasn't sure where from. As I began to repeat the information she was giving me about when and how she had passed, my eyes fell on people sitting to the right of me and I directed the information towards them, as I knew the spirit woman wanted to connect with one of them.

Lynne, a friend of mine, was sitting there and, as I looked at her, it suddenly dawned on me who the spirit woman was. I said, 'Oh my God, when did your mum die?'

I was a little bit rattled because I knew her mother very well. In fact she was president of the Spiritualist church in Aberdeen and I had stayed with her when I had served her church.

Lynne replied, 'On the date you just told us,' which had escaped my mind entirely in my moment of shock.

It felt a bit strange speaking to Mona, her mother, in the spirit world, as it was totally unexpected, but she had always liked to talk and her character hadn't changed. So, once I got over my surprise, I just allowed her to let rip and deliver her message to her daughter, which she did with great vigour.

At the end of the demonstration I spoke to Lynne, whom I hadn't actually seen for several years, and she was able to tell me what had happened. Before her mother had passed, she had given her a code that she would use when she came back to her through a medium, and she had said that she would try to use me as her medium if she could. During the message Lynne got her mother's code and she was delighted that it had come through me.

Both Lynne and her mother were Spiritualists and spiritual healers, but no matter how much belief you have, a loss can still hurt. This message, especially the personal content, allowed Lynne to truly begin to heal. We both had to laugh at how Mona had taken over the service, because even after I'd ended her message, I'd felt her spirit presence working with me as I gave messages to others, and at the end of the demonstration she made me go back to Lynne and apologise for saying she was dead – she was anything but dead!

The Determination of a Loving Son

Spirits aren't only very much alive on the other side, but when they have a love connection with us, space, time and distance are no barrier to communication. A friend and colleague, Simon James, sent me an account of one of the messages that came through his mediumship proving this:

While living in Victoria, BC, Canada, several years ago, I was asked to work in the Midlands of the UK.

Whilst there, in a demonstration I spoke to a lady about a young man who I felt had a connection back in BC. She understood this, as the young man was her cousin's son, who had not long passed away. I felt that he had died in an accident while mountaineering, and it so happened that he had died in an avalanche. I heard the names 'Michael' and 'Robin'; these were his name and the name of his climbing companion respectively. The contact was relatively short, but the main issue was that Michael's mother was grief-stricken and he was desperate to console her. The recipient said she would get in touch with her cousin and pass on the message.

Eight months later, I was working back home in Victoria, taking part in another demonstration, when I went to someone and gave pretty much the same information about the death of a young man in a climbing accident. I remember saying to the recipient that it was strange, but the young man felt similar to someone I had spoken about in the UK. It then transpired that it was the same contact and this person was a friend of the young man's mother! The same message was given – he wanted to console his mother in the depths of her grief. The friend said she was due to see the mother later that afternoon, as she lived in Victoria.

A month later the mother came to see me for a private consultation and there Michael was able to give evidence that he and his friend Robin had been overwhelmed by the avalanche and that he had survived in spirit if not in body. The mother thanked me for helping her to find some peace of mind, but I said it was little to do with me, but rather the persistence of her son trying to speak to me across two continents!

Hearing this account reminds me that there are so many true exponents of mediumship still working today. I also find it wonderful that the same spirit can communicate through the same medium to two separate people in two different lands and get his message delivered to his mother eventually.

I need no convincing of an afterlife, but I do hope that the messages I am able to share with you might make you look at the idea with at least an open mind, if nothing else.

I have heard it said that people who look for help from mediums after a loss are just holding on and this is unhealthy, but in all the years I have practised mediumship it has been my understanding that even if people don't go to mediums, they still talk to their loved ones after their passing and often refer to them when things are happening in the family. Is this kind of thing so wrong? I honestly believe that many people actually feel the presence of their beloved family and friends in the spirit world and that it is because of this sense that they are near to them that it feels normal to communicate with them.

I think it wise to point out that those in the spirit world don't see everything that we do, as such a thought might be disturbing, but there are moments when those we've loved or have loved us can draw close, usually when it is important to us. In both good and bad times, I believe they just wish to reassure us and let us know that we are never truly alone.

It is my wish, and that of any true medium, to try to show that there is more to life than meets the eye. If there had only been one or two accounts of spirits watching over us in this world then it would be easy to dismiss the idea that when we die, we die, but there have been millions of episodes in millions of people's lives – it is far more common than you might think. So, no, it's not wrong to talk to someone who was special to you after they pass, and honour their life and love, and please remember that at your lowest moments they will be watching over you and waiting for you to open up to them so that they can ease your grief and touch your mind with their love. After all, it is love that unlocks the door between the two worlds.

8

Incredible Messages

As a religion, the problem that Spiritualism has is that people can operate as mediums who are not part of the core movement and not fully trained, and some may be unscrupulous regarding the information they dish out. Also, it has allowed all those with psychic abilities, including mediums, to give readings for all sorts of things. So today people attend mediums seeking answers to their problems – in fact thinking that the spirit world will answer all their life's problems and give them perfect direction in matters of relationship and family and career, and so on.

As we've seen, there are times when a communicating spirit will offer information or advice about particular fears or concerns and may even give news of a positive outcome if it is allowed to be given, but we must remember that the spirit world cannot alleviate all our fears and steer us round all the pitfalls in life. We have to take responsibility for ourselves.

However, I know that spirits watch over us and if they get the opportunity will let us know that they are there for us. The lovely old medium Ivy Scott gave a splendid example of this type of message during her demonstration in a London church with me in 1996. She told a man in the congregation that his natural mother had been looking after him all his life, even though he had never been able to remember her. She told him that her name was Betty and that she had died while having him. This was true, according to the recipient. Then she said that his mother had been with him on the 24th of that month when he had been in hospital for tests. He again accepted this. In her quick-fire style, Ivy described other moments from his life that his mother had seen, like his wedding day and the birth of his children and other important events he felt she had missed out on.

At the close of this short message, she told him that he must tell Sylvia that his mother thanked her for everything she had done for her son. The man said that Sylvia was the lady who had brought him up and that he would do just as his mother had told him.

Like the Reverend Kennedy in his search for proof after his wife's passing, most people want to test the spirits, but as time has gone on I've often found that they prove things to us just as in this example, without prompts or demands.

Let me share some more incredible messages with you.

'How Could Anyone Know That?'

Several years ago, when I was working in London, I was asked if I would sit with a gentleman who had come to the Spiritualist church searching for a medium who might help him. When you work for churches, you aren't given any information about private sitters prior to their visit, so that was all I was told.

I waited in the small healing chapel where the private sittings were conducted and I remember that the man called and told the secretary that he was running late, so I just meditated for a while.

On his arrival, I noticed that he looked very flustered. He

apologised for his lateness, but made no mention of what had held him up. He must have been in his late forties or early fifties, I reckoned. He was tall and dark-haired with a sallow complexion that made him look as though he came from one of the Mediterranean countries, but I wouldn't hazard a guess as to which, and he spoke in a very clear English accent.

Rather than speculate about what sort of man he might be, I began the sitting by explaining what might happen during our session. Moments later I could sense the presence of a young woman in the spirit world who seemed to want to communicate urgently.

As I described her from the mental picture that was forming in my mind, I could see that the man was very interested in what I was telling him. He accepted the description I gave him and soon afterwards I started an inner dialogue with the spirit, who informed me that she was his daughter, she had died less than a year ago, and she had met her end in a terrible car accident in Australia of all places.

The man nodded his head in acceptance and I carried on speaking. His daughter gave him very personal information and I can say that he understood everything he was hearing. It was as the sitting was closing that I heard her voice coming through much more strongly, and as clear as day she said, 'Dad, I just saw you deliver that baby. I was with you then and I will always try to be near you when I can.'

The man burst into a fit of laughter that made tears of joy run down his face. He told me that he was a doctor in one of the London hospitals and that there had been an emergency with one of his patients and he had had to perform a Caesarean section or the baby might not have lived.

I remember being quite shocked when I heard this because,

as a medium, you often hear the words coming from your mouth, but you never really know what they mean until the sitter explains it all to you.

As for the doctor, this blew him away – he just couldn't work out how anyone could have known what he'd just done. He'd already received many pieces of accurate information about his daughter's life and death, but it was this that really made him wonder.

Could it have been telepathy? This has often been suggested. In fact, in more than 100 years of psychical research, investigators have often fallen back on telepathy as an explanation when they have been unable to account for something a medium has done.

My doctor struggled to find another explanation. Somehow, he was able to accept that a medium might be able to tell a relative things about the life of a deceased person, but he had never reckoned that the deceased themselves might still be participating in the here and now. I remember discussing the possibilities with him: either I was a mind-reader, which in itself was not the norm, or the consciousness of his daughter was still able to see into his life and report things about it.

The good doctor left the little healing chapel that day with more new questions about life and death than he'd bargained for.

'But This Is Incredible!'

Spirits can not only see into our lives but also, as we have already seen, offer assistance at crucial times. When we find ourselves in difficulties and this world seems too much to bear, we naturally look upwards for spiritual help, and yet I believe that the 'up' of the spiritual world is in frequency rather than location.

It is my understanding that spirits are higher than us in vibration and in luminosity. By this I mean that they are composed of something far less dense than the human body, though our mind can interact with theirs and we can be helped by guidance from these higher sources.

I have heard so many accounts from people who would no more think of spirit worlds than fly, yet have had experiences which have included inner or outer voices offering assistance to carry them through their difficult moments.

I gave a reading one time to a young man who came to me in London shortly after his sister's tragic passing. He had lost several people in his life and was suffering from depression. I remember how embarrassed he looked as he entered the hotel room we met in. He couldn't make eye contact and he spoke very little, giving a one-word reply when I asked him if he had sat with a medium before. Immediately my heart went out to him, as he could only have been in his thirties and he was tall and good-looking and yet so heavy in mind. I tried to get him to relax, then I began to tune in.

With no prior knowledge of his loss, straightaway I began to describe his sister and her recent tragic passing. She had taken her own life after a bout of serious depression, which the family seemed not to have noticed. Therefore they all, including her brother, were feeling a lot of guilt. I described how and when she died and she gave many details, which I could tell had caught the man's attention, as his demeanour began to change and he looked more alert than when he had first entered the room.

Then another spirit joined the message, a young man who had been the man's friend and had been shot some years earlier. He gave his name, which was one I had never heard before, but my sitter accepted it, though with a look of sheer astonishment on his face.

Then he gave a message which astonished even me: 'I was the one who saved your life last Christmas. It was my voice you heard. I saved you because you have great work to do.'

The young man facing me began to cry and laugh all at the same time and said, 'But this is incredible! How can this be?'

This statement lifted him to a state of bewilderment and excitement at the same time. I carried on with the reading and several other things came through, then we spent time afterwards just talking and I did my best to explain to him that, as the medium, I only passed on the messages, and that often I knew nothing more than what was being said. It is not unusual for a sitter to assume that a medium knows more than they are saying because they have made several correct statements, but more often than not the medium is just reporting, not interpreting.

Later on, the man wanted me to have dinner with him, as he said he needed to tell me about the message, and I did, as I was now curious to hear his story.

At dinner he explained that while he'd been on holiday in Sri Lanka with his young family the previous Christmas, staying in a beautiful hotel on the beach, he'd heard a voice telling him to change hotels. How can you hear a voice out of nowhere? The man didn't understand it, as there hadn't been anyone else with him at the time, but his background was very academic and he tried to think it through logically. He was also perturbed because with the voice came a very strong feeling of impending danger.

Getting nowhere with trying to explain it all, at first he ignored it and tried to carry on with his holiday, but as the day wore on he began to feel sick inside. Finally, he decided to act on his feelings and started searching for another hotel just to see what would happen. He found one on the other side of the island which seemed to offer a lot for very little, and, thinking this was almost too good to be true, he moved his family that day. Instantly the feeling of danger disappeared.

The family enjoyed a wonderful Christmas Day in their new accommodation and the following morning the man and his partner woke to peace and quiet. Both went out on the balcony to enjoy the morning and looked out onto the calm empty sea before them.

In a moment of complete horror, they both realised that the sea should not have been there and, still not sure what had happened, they ran to look for the children. They found them playing happily on the rooftop by the swimming pool, totally oblivious to the fact that one of the worst natural disasters in modern history had just occurred. It was that terrible tsunami of Boxing Day 2004 that took hundreds of thousands of lives.

I was gripped just listening to the man's account of his experience. It was now clear to me why he was so astonished by the statement made during his reading.

I can reveal that he has since gone on to do many great things through his work and has helped hundreds of thousands of people in his country. Who knows, he may go on to help millions.

That would have been reason enough for someone from the spirit world to speak to him at that moment. But there must also have been something in the atmosphere around him that allowed his beloved friend on the other side to breach the veil between the two worlds to get the message across. As I said earlier, more research might lead to greater understanding of spirit communication.

Helen and her Friend

Earlier I mentioned Mrs Helen Hughes and said that I never got to meet her, but in a certain way I did. In the summer of 2000, when I was giving readings at the Spiritualist Association of Great Britain in London's Belgrave Square, I met a very lovely elderly lady from India who came to me for a private reading. I remember noticing that even in old age she had a real beauty and dignity.

During the reading I mentioned to her that her friend Helen wanted to communicate with her and was saying she remembered saving her life. When I made this statement, the woman looked at me, gave a very warm smile and said, 'Oh my God, you have Helen Hughes with you then.'

I was quite astounded, because Helen was one of my inspirations.

The lady told me that on her first meeting with Helen she had been struck by her accuracy, and Helen had even spoken to her in her own language at times while delivering a message to her. Shortly after this first encounter she had invited her to India so that she might help some of her friends who had lost loved ones. After this first visit she and Helen had become firm friends and remained so until Helen's passing in 1976.

Not long after Helen had died, the lady had been travelling in a car in India. The journey had already taken several hours and, sitting in the back seat, she had laid her head against the window and drifted into a light sleep. She hadn't noticed that her driver had become tired and also drifted into a light sleep.

Then she had quite clearly dreamed of Helen. She could see her face looking at her and suddenly she heard her scream out to her, in her own voice, '*Wake up and sit up!*'

This command jolted her body upright from her slumped position in the back of the car, just as there was a crash and the window she had been resting against smashed into pieces as a large rock broke through, exactly where her head had been.

Her driver was out of his door in seconds, pulling at her to get her out of the wreck. They had veered into a massive rock pile by the side of the dusty road they had been travelling along.

It was a moment that she had never forgotten, and though many of her loved ones came through in that reading with me, it was the message from Helen that pleased her most. As she said to me, even in the spirit world her friend was looking after her and helping her.

I believe that when we make a bond with another person, be it family or friend, when that bond is true and loving, it can never be broken. Though these two women came from very different backgrounds and lived on opposite sides of the world, their affection for each other was greater than distance or even death. It is this type of bond that reaches beyond human understanding.

For me, this message was a true gift from the spirit world, because it allowed me a moment inside the mind and life of someone I had never met because of the passage of time. It allowed me to sense her spirit, which defied time itself.

Have Faith

I believe that we all have a sense that there is someone watching over us. I don't think it matters if you feel that these guardians take the form of angelic beings, spirit guides or loved ones, God himself or a special deity. Whether you put your stock in Jesus, Mohammed or Buddha, you are looking up to a higher force than yourself, and such thinking means that you are already practising raising your vibration – lifting your spirit to a higher frequency while you're here on Earth.

A hairdresser I once worked with called Amerina told me that she kept getting the feeling that there was something wrong with her car. It became so strong that she was actually starting to be afraid of getting into it. Even though she had her mechanic thoroughly inspect the vehicle and it appeared to be perfectly safe, the feeling persisted.

Thinking that she was just paranoid, she did her best to push the feeling away, but there was always a nagging doubt in her mind about the car. I recall that she said it even felt as though someone was speaking to her when she got the feeling, but she couldn't quite make out who it was.

Then, while driving home from a friend's house one night, she drove onto a bridge crossing the River Clyde and had just put her foot down to pick up enough speed to merge with the flowing traffic when her gut went into a knot and a loud voice that sounded like her grandmother's called out for her to slow down. She reacted instinctively, and a good job too. The back wheel of her car sheared off and sent the car hurtling towards the edge of the bridge. It only just stopped short of the barrier between her and the drop into the river. If she had been travelling any faster, she would have ended up in the Clyde.

Her question to me was, could this really have been her relative in the spirit world trying to save her life? For me it was a given. As a medium, I am certain that a force from the other side was watching over her and in fact saved her from a very nasty accident.

I must add that it is not only warnings of impending doom or gloom that come through in messages. There are so many occasions when we are alerted to good news or special events that are about to happen too. I honestly believe that the important thing to look at here is not just the message, but the fact that it might have come from someone you thought of as no longer living.

Lost in Translation

I have already mentioned Rosalind Cattanach, who wrote the book on the life of Albert Best. I got to know Ros, as she was more commonly known, in 1994 when I was first asked to work at the Spiritualist church she ran in Notting Hill Gate in west London. Over the years we became friends. Even though there were many years between us, we found we could sit and converse about life for hours, often over a glass of good scotch.

One Friday night when I arrived at her home above the church, she asked me if I knew of a Scottish medium called Jean Glenn. I told her that I did and that I thought Jean a very good medium, and then asked her why she was enquiring.

She told me that several weeks before, while she had been going about her business, sorting out things for the church, she had heard a voice telling her to go and see Jean Glenn. She remarked that she had no idea who this was or why she had heard such a thing, for though she ran the church, she never felt that she had any mediumship gifts herself, and the whole thing seemed quite odd.

Nevertheless, she began to make enquiries, as she had a feeling that Jean Glenn might be a medium she had never heard of. Her thinking was if Jean came recommended by other churches, she might book her to serve her own church, but other than that she wasn't too concerned about the message.

Ros found that Jean was working at the SAGB in London and called to book a private reading with her, using her sister's name, as she felt that because she ran a church, mediums might have heard of her, even if they hadn't met her, and this might influence the reading.

I enquired how the reading had gone, at which point Ros seemed quite perturbed. She said that Jean had appeared to be a very nice woman, but she had left the reading feeling disappointed because other than a few correct names, none of it had meant anything to her. This baffled me, as I knew that Jean was an excellent medium and if she couldn't get anything proper, she would stop the session. Good mediums know when it's not working and won't carry on just for the sake of things.

I asked Ros more about it and she said that because of Jean's accent she felt that she'd missed a lot of what was being said, but she hadn't wanted to keep cutting in to stop her, as every now and then she had made out something that sounded correct, only to lose the next part.

I then asked if she had taped the session, which she had, so I asked her if she would mind me listening to it and trying to make it clearer for her, as it was much easier for me to understand a Scottish accent than it was for her. She agreed and played the recording back for me.

The sitting began with Jean telling Ros not to feed her information, that she, the medium, was there to give information to her, the sitter. She said a short prayer to lift her mind to the spirit world and then told Ros that Alan was there. Alan was the name of Ros's husband. He's 'goat offy shaky hands', as Jean put it, and Alan's hands had shaken a lot because of Parkinson's. So I knew that Jean was presenting accurate information.

As I listened to the reading and translated each statement for Ros, she became fascinated. She told me that she had never heard any of this while it was happening. Jean had gone on to give her the name of her son David, who, she said, had died at the age of eighteen in an accident. She commented, 'This wiz the wurst July of yur life, wiz it no?' Translated, that meant David had died in the month of July, which was true. Ros dreaded every anniversary.

But this was just evidence that Ros's family were communicating with her. The crux of the reading was that her spirit family was warning her that there were people on the committee of her church who were secretly trying to oust her from her position as president and therefore from her home – the medium gave the names of every one of them.

Ros was shocked to hear this, but not totally surprised. However, according to the advice that came through, she would have to act fast to save her position and her home.

Jean's closing statement came from an old friend of Ros's called Nan, who claimed she had told her to go for this sitting with this medium.

'Well, I never!' Ros exclaimed. It was Nan who had been talking to her! She hadn't recognised her voice at the time, but Nan had been as big a part of that church as she was now. Suddenly the whole thing made sense.

Ros was so grateful for her message that she immediately put pen to paper to apologise to Jean Glenn for appearing so vague during the reading and to thank her for the amazing information that had truly helped her. She was lifted to new heights by the thought that her old friend Nan had found a way to alert her from the spirit world about goings on that were taking place under her nose; it made her feel cared for and protected in some way.

You see, people don't always know when the spirit world is guiding them because they look for the obvious, when often they are being warned about the things they would never imagine. I am certain that many people are guided away from bad or sad things that they never even know about – how could they, if they don't experience them?

'Did Something Else Happen?'

On another occasion I was asked to attend a woman who told me she just wanted me to give her some healing after receiving the bad news from her doctor that she had a very short time to live. This lady had become friendly with me during her many operations for cancer and had actually gone into remission for a time after previous healing sessions, so when I got this request, I was shocked to say the least.

I remember going to her home in Glasgow and sitting talking with her and listening to how she wanted everything to be at the end of her life. She instructed me to give her a healing session, not to try to cure her, but to relax her mind so she could muster the strength to carry out her final duties before she became too infirm.

This was another of those moments in my mediumship when my trust in the higher mind of spirit was put to the test. As I was standing behind my friend to give her the healing, I sensed the presence of a man in the spirit world. Now I wasn't there to give her a message, but the presence became so strong that soon I could identify the person. It was Albert Best, who had not long passed to the spirit world.

In the quiet of my own mind, I asked, 'Why are you here, Albert?'

Albert was a great healer as well as a medium, as you know, but somehow I never thought for a moment that he had come to perform healing. And he hadn't. He had come to give a message.

In my own inner thinking, I heard him clearly say, 'She is not dying.'

This totally threw me, as it was the last thing I expected to hear.

I asked how he knew this and the words came into my mind in a second: 'It's all a big mistake.'

I wanted something else from Albert to prove this, and even as I thought that, I could hear his voice in my head telling me that the lady had received a letter that morning from her brother, whom she hadn't spoken to in years, and he began to describe the contents of the letter to me. The message ended with him saying, 'If she confirms this to you, tell her she is not dying just yet.'

Okay, try to imagine this situation. You have a woman you are friendly with, a woman whom you have witnessed being seriously ill at times and going through all sorts of operations and treatments, and who is now telling you that her consultant has told her she only has weeks to live, and you have a spirit voice telling you otherwise.

I have always discouraged healers and mediums from giving medical diagnoses or advice to people, because we are not medically trained. Also, it would be awful to offer this woman false hope; something else I would never advocate, but that was where I was at that moment.

At the end of the healing session, I didn't know what to do. I just sat quietly and let the lady tell me how she felt, which was much more relaxed and clear-headed and so on. But she knew me quite well. She looked at me curiously and said, 'Did something else happen that you're not telling me?'

I couldn't think what to say.

She broke into a smile and continued, as if to encourage me, 'Gordon, there's nothing you could say to me at this moment that would shock me.'

Oh, but there was. If only she knew what I had just heard and from whom.

I was honestly reluctant to share anything with her. I thought I would just brush it off and keep it all to myself, and that way she would be none the wiser. Either she would pass and not know, or, if what I had been told did turn out to be true, she would feel great again at some point. So it would be fine either way.

Just then a surge of energy passed through my body and I said out loud, 'You received a letter this morning from so-and-so, who is your brother, and it said blah blah blah.'

I literally repeated word for word what Albert had told me, including that it was all a big mistake.

Finally, I blurted out, 'Ten days from now, you will know.'

I remember thinking, 'Oh no, I've said it!', even though in a way *I* hadn't said anything, because at that moment my mind had been totally connected to Albert in the spirit world and he had told her through me. Still, it had been said.

The lady just burst out laughing and couldn't stop – not because she believed me, but because she thought I was so sympathetic that I was trying to give her a sense of hope. She explained that it was okay and she wasn't upset by it. We knew each other and she was taking it in her stride. She really wasn't bothered by it, even though she *was* astounded by the word for word description I had given of the letter from her brother.

I told her I was sorry and I'd never done anything like that before and hoped never to again. I explained that it had been Albert who had given me the information, but she even brushed that off. She was aware of Albert's great mediumship, of course, but we both agreed that that would explain the accuracy of the letter and left it at that.

Ten days later she called me, in fits of laughter again, only this time because her consultant had called her in and apologised to her, as he had looked at the wrong files on her previous visit and it had all been a very big and bad mistake. He was horrified, and my friend could have taken this mix-up further, but this medical team had saved her life on many occasions before, and she was just so relieved to have her reprieve.

I was also relieved. Though I worked out that the spirits had been testing me to see how much I trusted them with something this close to the edge, I asked them *never* to do it again, and they never have – well, not in that way. This type of message helps build your trust as a medium, but I would much rather not have to go out on that kind of limb if I don't have to.

One good thing, at least, was that Albert showed me that even beyond the grave he was still able to communicate good news to people.

This happened around 1997 and, as far as I'm aware, the lady is still alive today.

9

What Happens When We Die?

I think that everyone alive in this world will at some point look at the question of what lies beyond this life for us. If you have a strong religious faith, then you might not fear death. But there must surely be millions of people living today who ponder on life and death and fall short of answers because they feel that nothing satisfies their need by way of proof or even evidence of continued existence.

During my life I have seen, heard and experienced so many proofs that there is continued life after the physical journey that I honestly don't even question it any more. This knowledge has taken most of the fears of this life from my mind, and over the years it has been my pleasure to give talks on the subject of life after death and help others lift their thinking to a higher level where fear cannot disturb them.

I will always remember meeting a young man called Dan, who told me that he was twenty-three years old and that he couldn't remember a night in his young adult life when he'd been able to go to sleep peacefully for thinking about dying. He'd lie there tossing and turning, fearing his death. It was such an amazing thing to hear him also tell me that after attending a talk I gave on the afterlife and watching a demonstration of mediumship I gave, he felt that he was fighting back against the fear.

It is when I hear stories like this that I realise that the years

I have put into my development have been worth it. As much as many of the messages people get from mediums is personal and can help on that level, I truly believe that the bigger message is what Dan experienced – a sense of something larger that is there to help us get over the fear of living and dying.

Looking through the Window

Ever since the day I first walked into Mrs Primrose's church some thirty-odd years ago, I have sat with a small group of friends once a week whenever possible to communicate with the spirit world. In Spiritualist terms we call it our 'circle'. In this circle we learn to lift our minds through meditation to a higher state where a guiding spirit can bond with us and impart experience and information from the other side. This can be a guiding spirit or just spirit guiding us – personality isn't needed at a certain stage of development.

In whatever form, the guides will often teach us about ourselves and our lives and even how to adjust our minds to blend with the spirit state, which is what will happen to all of us when we eventually leave our physical body and pass from this world to the next. It was during one of our sessions that I was given a very rare opportunity to experience what it feels like to leave this life and move on.

I believe that this was in the winter of 2014, as I hadn't long moved back to Scotland after living for eleven years in London, and I was sitting in my circle with the friends I had sat with years earlier.

During our circle we often send out prayers and healing

intentions for people we have heard about in the previous week who need help or who have asked us to help others. That particular week I had been asked by a woman I had met in Switzerland if I could help her, as she had been told that she was dying and she was very afraid. What she had specifically asked was if our circle could pray for her not to be afraid when the time came.

Our small group of five people sat around my front room and shared the information we had been asked to take into our meditation time. Then we went into the silence of the room. This was followed by all of us feeling the power of spirit vibrating around us and lifting our minds to a higher state of being. I think I will always remember that moment, because what happened to me next was beyond words, though I will do my best to describe what I experienced.

First of all, there was a pulsing around my chest area that got stronger and faster. I didn't feel fazed by this, because it is quite common for me to feel this type of sensation when going into an altered state of consciousness. It would have been quite normal for me to have sensed the presence of my spirit guide at that moment, but instead I felt that I was expanding out from my physical body and filling every inch of the room I was sitting in.

My conscious mind was still alert, but on a different level from anything I can truly explain in words. I could see, hear and feel the people in the room with me, but my senses were so amplified that I could hear their thoughts and feel their individual heartbeats. It was as if I was all of them at once. I was aware of this, but not concerned by it or fixated on it. I knew that I was continuing on to something and somewhere else.

Somehow, though I could feel I was still connected to the

people, the room and what was going on in it, at the same time I was in another realm of existence. The Swiss lady I had been sending prayers for was standing somewhere in this realm, which seemed lighter than the world I had come from and not separate from it, but defined as different by a tone or vibration, rather than a boundary or dividing line. It's not easy to describe. There were no real images as such, more sensations and impressions. But I could tell the Swiss lady was smiling and looking far better than I had ever seen her look. She was younger in a way that made her seem as though she was radiating a light even brighter than the place of light we were both in.

In a moment that was less than a second of time, I heard her say that Bruno was with her and that she had to leave him behind, but she knew it was right. Though I could hear her speaking, it seemed her lips never moved. She then spoke to her mother and father and someone called Anna, and I could make out three figures of light moving towards her. At that very moment I felt an amazing sensation of freedom and release. I know I'm not doing anything like justice to it with this description, but I will remember it for ever with every cell of my body.

It was almost over, but for a moment I felt that I was in something like a skin or fine membrane of light material. I seemed to know that in order to be where I was and experience another person going into the spirit world, I had to be contained within something that allowed me to be there but not there, as it were. In a way I suppose it was like wearing a suit for deep-sea diving. I had a sense that I was there for a moment, but also only observing from behind a window or something. I did say it was hard to explain!

What I can tell you for sure is that the following day I was called by my friend Pia from Switzerland, who had connected me with the lady who was dying, and, without knowing what I had experienced the previous evening, she told me that the lady had died that evening in her husband Bruno's arms, and she had died with a smile on her face. It had been just after eight o'clock, which would have been just after seven our time in the UK. That was exactly when I had been sitting in my circle having that experience.

It just made me smile to myself, because I know that lady had that amazing feeling of freedom and release, and when we die, we will have it too.

I have had similar experiences of dying, but there was a much finer quality to that one that really showed me that the death we will all go through at some point will feel like an expansion once we step away from our human connection to fear.

I also feel that I was allowed to observe the soul passing to the spirit world but not actually allowed to be in the spirit world itself, and that is why I felt separate from it.

No matter what your belief or faith, or even if you have none, it is my understanding that we will all be met on the other side and we will all expand and grow just after that moment of letting go of our physical body and, in no time at all, all will become clear to us.

Walking Part of the Way with Someone You Love

Near the end of my father's life, he experienced many serious episodes of illness that almost took him to the other side. Each time this happened I would get a sense that it wasn't his time and something inside me would feel content. I was living in London at the time. Then, during one of these episodes, everything inside me told me to go to him and be with him.

One of the things that I thank the spirit world for is a sort of early warning system that kicks in when I can be of use to someone I care about. It was because of this that I was able to spend the last week of my father's life by his side. We would sit in his living room, with him upright in his chair, his mind often wandering between the two worlds. When he was conscious enough, we would talk, and he would tell me that he had had an experience in which he had met his younger sister, who had died many years before. He told me that he had felt that he was in a room filled with light and that all his infirmities had seemed to disappear for that moment.

I didn't want my father to have any fear of death, so I spoke to him about everything that was happening to him. This was a man who had taught me how to tie my shoelaces, how to tie a knot in my tie, and how to be brave and strong if I fell down as a child. I wanted him to feel safe in my care when he needed it.

When his consciousness would fade and his body would appear lifeless, I would hold his hand and take my mind into a trance state. That way I felt that I could be with him in this in-between place. Then, as soon as I felt the life-force coming back into his body and I knew it wasn't his time, I would bring myself back too. He would tell me that he could feel me by his side, as if I was walking somewhere with him. I told him that I was, and after that he would always relax and sleep normally for a few hours.

On the last morning of his earthly life he asked me if I

could get him to a hospice and, between us, my sister Betty and I did just that. Once he was settled, I sat with him and told him that if he looked out of his window that night he would see the city light up and one light in particular would guide him home. And I assured him that I would walk with him as far as I could.

My father was such a strong man. No matter what life dished out to him, he found a way to handle it. His last conversation with me in this life was to tell me to go home to London, as he didn't need me any more. He asked for my mother and all the family to come and say their goodbyes, but he knew that I could walk with him when the time came no matter where I was.

It was true. I was sitting on the train heading to London that evening, just after all the family had visited him, when I heard the voice of my guide say, 'It's time to walk with your father.'

I closed my eyes, listened to the sound of the train chuntering along, found its rhythm and followed it until in my inner sight I saw the city of Glasgow, now far behind me yet in the forefront of my mind, and I could feel myself walking as if on magical air above it, and by my side was my father, getting younger with every step he took.

My mind went into a sort of light sleep state until I was jolted out of my meditation by the sound of my mobile phone ringing loudly in the quiet carriage. It was my sister telling me Dad had gone. I told her I knew. She said that a nurse and a doctor had sat with him in his final moments and he had whispered that he had to walk into the lights and had turned on his left side, facing the city where he was born and bred.

The next time I heard from him was the night before his

funeral, when he whispered to me and showed me a vision of things that would spontaneously happen at his funeral. Everything came true. He had learned that if I could walk beside him in that in-between state, he could return the compliment.

I honestly never grieved the death of my father; we had completed a journey together in life and beyond, something I thank the spirit guides for teaching me.

Summerland

I had the most wonderful experience in a session of trance mediumship recently, when I was giving a demonstration to a small gathering in Switzerland. In this dreamlike state, I felt my consciousness leave my body, and while this was happening, my guide was using my body and operating my voice to speak to one of the people present about her son, who had tragically died in a shooting incident.

I was able to hear the voice of the guide speaking, but it seemed to be way in the distance, or echoing through a megaphone somewhere far away. At the same moment I was aware of a young man standing beside me, talking to me, yet his mouth wasn't moving. It was as if we were speaking from our souls in a language of telepathy that did not require a mouth.

Again, I honestly have no words that would do justice to the sensation I was experiencing. It was beyond my under-standing. 'There's a land that is fairer than day' is the opening line of an old hymn we would sing in Mrs Primrose's church, and I felt as if I was in such a place.

Those who were watching and listening to the trance were

hooked on the message that was being given to the woman about her son and the description of his new spiritual life or state of being. My guide, Chi, was explaining that on his death he had felt no pain, but a sense of acceleration, a heightening of the senses, and almost instantly he had been out of his body.

'The medium,' he said, referring to me, 'is now experiencing the same moment that your son did, and you will see when he is fully back with you how it affects him.'

Chi then told the group that this was what they would all experience. No matter how they passed out of this life, each one would lighten in mind, vibration and luminosity.

He explained that death was just an experience of change. It was the change that they all feared, because it was in their thinking to do so, but if they could be sure of this change, they would live a life of less fear and less struggle on the road to death and beyond.

The woman's father then communicated, saying that he was with her son and that they were both free and completely at peace in the spirit existence. He talked to his daughter directly, using my voice, and told her that she had to accept her son's death, as guilt and regret would only hold her mind in a dark prison and that wasn't what either he or her son wished for the rest of her life on Earth. The message was given in a very gentle and loving way, which made the woman cry, but the sounds that left her body indicated release more than pain.

At the close of this session I felt myself becoming aware of the room and as I slowly opened my eyes, I found the whole gathering was staring at me. My face was wet with tears – tears of pure joy. It was as if I was glowing in some way and I honestly found it hard to speak for a moment. I had got a glimpse of the spirit world, and though it didn't have structure as we know it, there was a sense of life there that was greater than anything I had ever felt – and I have had some amazing spiritual experiences.

The woman who had received the message came over to me and asked if she could hug me, and I said, 'Of course.' In that embrace it felt as though she shared a moment of the experience I had had, and I believe it helped her to understand that her son wasn't stuck somewhere, but was free. As the guide had explained to her, it is only the emotions of our human condition that can hold us back, and her son was in his spirit body.

I believe I got to experience, albeit only for a moment, my own spirit body, and it was a moment of rejoicing, not fear. Though I haven't the words anyway, it was like being in a land that is fairer than day.

The Unbreakable Bond

Earlier I mentioned Rosalind Cattanach, who wrote books on the lives of Nan Mackenzie and Albert Best. Several years ago she allowed me to listen to a tape-recording of Albert while he was in a trance state and his guides and her son David, who you remember had died at the age of eighteen, were speaking to her directly.

It was the most amazing session of mediumship. A male voice spoke through Albert in an accent that I knew wasn't his. Also, the voice was very clear and concise in manner, whereas Albert tended to bumble a bit when he talked. So I knew it was the voice of one of the spirit guides who worked with him.

The guide told Ros that her son was standing beside him. He gave details about where and when he had died and many small pieces of personal evidence, all of which she accepted. Then the guide, using Albert's hand, pointed to a cabinet in her living room, where the sitting was taking place, and said, 'In this cabinet there is a small black case that once belonged to your boy. If you look in that case you will see a photograph of your son standing on the front of a small boat called the *Sea Wing*. This picture was the last that was ever taken of him. There is also a card tucked into a small pouch in the wallet that shows that your son donated blood two weeks before his death.'

There was so much information coming through that Ros was finding it hard to think straight, but she knew that her son's possessions had been put in the cabinet that the guide had mentioned. It was locked and she hadn't ever wanted to look at her son's things, but she knew that she would be able to check later. She didn't think that David would have given blood without mentioning it to her, though.

After all the evidence, the voice changed to that of a younger man, who spoke in a much more cultured way than Albert usually did.

'Mother, Mother, it's me, David. I wanted you to know that I am with you and I know what has happened to Father.'

Ros's husband had been diagnosed with Parkinson's disease just weeks before.

David continued, 'It's amazing that I can speak to you again and I need you to know that I am in a great place, a state of something else, if you like, Mother. I find it difficult to describe when I have to use words again, but it's fantastic.'

There was a pause on the tape for a moment and then David started to speak again.

'Mother,' he said, 'I want you to know that I can be with you whenever you think of me. We are connected – we will always be connected, nothing can change that – and no matter how my consciousness grows and expands, no matter how far my mind moves away from the idea of a physical body, I can always be near you in just one thought. It feels as though there is a bond between us that keeps us connected, a thread if you will, that allows me to know what you're feeling and thinking at times, and yet there is no time now where I am. Isn't it incredible, Mother?'

I remember as I listened to the tape, all thoughts of Albert Best being involved in this dialogue left my mind. It was like hearing a completely different man speak with an enthusiasm that I can only explain as exuberant. Other things were said, which were more personal to Ros, but it was the description of the other side from David's point of view that grabbed me – how he talked about expanding and growing in consciousness, rather than giving a description of a spirit world, which is how many of the old Spiritualist books refer to the afterlife. Also, how he said that there was always a connection that could come into use if needed. I would assume that he meant that he had an existence of sorts beyond human understanding, but if the need arose he could be close to his mother and sense her in some way.

Having experienced trance states myself, which cause you to feel disconnected from your own body for a period, I can understand what David was referring to. Each time I have experienced that state, I have had no sense of time, no sense of body, yet still have felt an individual, albeit in a higher, more refined state of mind. As David explains, or tries to explain, in this message to his mother, there just aren't words to describe what it feels like when you are out of your human self.

The first part of the message, about David's possessions, was also quite something. This was the first message Albert had given to Ros – they hardly knew each other at this time – and he had never been in her front room before that day. Her husband had hidden the key to the cabinet after he had locked his son's possessions away, and Ros told me later that it had taken her a full day to find it, as he'd actually forgotten where he'd put it. It had finally turned up in an upstairs wardrobe in a small box within a larger box.

Ros had never wanted to look at her son's things, for fear of bringing back painful memories, but now she opened the cabinet and found the small black attaché case mentioned by the guide. She opened it to see a picture of David standing on the bow of a small white sailing boat with the name *Sea Wing* painted on the front, exactly as described. She told me that she was totally amazed by this, but then she was even more astounded when she pushed her fingers into the little wallet and felt a plastic card inside. When she pulled it out, it revealed her son's name and the fact that he had given blood two weeks before his untimely death.

This account never appeared in Ros's book on Albert's life. She thought that people simply wouldn't believe it. Not only did she hear what she totally believed to be her son's voice describing his unbreakable bond with her, but she had amazing evidence of it as well.

As for Albert, he just did this kind of thing over and over, without thought of reward or praise.

Farewell, Not Goodbye

Many people ask me if I miss Albert and I always tell them that he hasn't gone entirely, he still pops up from time to time – like the time he came and told me about the mistake when the lady had been told she was going to die. You see, between some people, bonds of true friendship are formed that can never be broken, and that, I believe, is the case with Albert and me.

There have been many times when I've been giving messages and felt someone close by and have known it's him by what comes out of my mouth. On one such occasion I was giving a message to a lady in a packed theatre and out of nowhere I began to describe the contents of her handbag, something that Albert did often, much to people's amusement.

On another occasion, he showed up in a dream I was having early one morning. It was one of those prophetic dreams that seems very real, and there was Albert looking at me and showing me a house in a lovely part of Scotland. Though I lived in England at the time, he told me it was my house. Two years later I found that house and live there still. Before that dream I had never even thought about living in that area.

In the few years after I became friends with Albert Best, I learned more about the man than the medium. I learned that he did all his good work, like so many others mentioned in this book, for the good of others and not for monetary gain. I learned that after the loss of his young wife and three small kids in 1944, he carried a weight in his heart that even with all his experience he couldn't rid himself of. So I learned he would do anything to help those who had lost children and were carrying great grief inside. It was a true mission for him and I can understand why. And, just like Mrs

Primrose, he was as honest as the day is long and always displayed humility and kindness towards other people.

On 2 April 1996, Albert slipped into a coma after suffering a stroke and was taken to hospital. He was there for several days. Each night I would go to his bedside and hold his hand, along with my partner, Jim, and Albert's friend Ann. Each night we would sit around his bed and talk quietly about all the amazing things we knew he had done, and though he never responded, we all believed that somewhere he could hear us and was laughing.

For ten days he remained in his coma and then on 12 April, as I held his hand, Jim, who was standing on the opposite side of his bed, did the same, and Ann, who was standing beside me, put her hand on his forehead. We never spoke that time, just sent our thoughts and prayers to our friend, and each of us was asking for him to be released from this in-between state to go home to spirit.

Then something began to happen that made the three of us look to the bottom of the bed. There was a sort of pulse, if you like, but nothing we could see. For just a moment I thought I was seeing a build-up of energy – not like ecto-plasm, just light changing and moving – but neither of the others could see this.

Just then Albert opened his eyes and looked first at Ann and then at Jim and finally at me as he whispered, 'They're here – my wife and children are here.'

His eyes then locked on the empty space at the bottom of the bed where I had thought I could see the energy moving.

'You'll have to let me go now,' he said.

I thought none of us would be able to get words out of our mouths, but Ann did, saying simply, 'We were never holding you, Albert.'

The intensity around his bed was similar to that experienced when going into a trance. For a moment we thought the room was vibrating, as Albert smiled and we let go of him.

I have no idea what happened next, when Albert's doctor went in to examine him, but he said the strangest thing to me afterwards: 'I don't know what that man did, but I get a feeling that the world has lost a very special person.'

He could hardly speak for the great lump in his throat and his eyes were streaming with tears. Who knows, maybe my old friend found the strength to do one last message for the road before his fond farewell.

Taxi Home

In the spring of 2004 I was asked to present a special evening of mediumship with Mrs Duffy in the Spiritualist church in Albany Street in Edinburgh. As I mentioned earlier, I always liked to work with this lovely medium, for she brought a brightness to her demonstrations that lifted the congregation.

That night was no exception. She began her first message with, 'Darling, I wish to speak to a couple who are sitting right at the back of the church. The name "Urquhart" is written right above your heads.'

A couple at the back both spoke, saying that was their name.

'You have a daughter in the spirit world who sadly lost her fight to cancer last year and she wishes to speak with you. Would that be alright?'

Mrs Duffy went on to give them a beautiful message from their daughter, who thanked them for all they had done for her during her illness and for how they were helping her husband and children in the here and now.

The evening went on like this, with messages coming through both Mary and me, until we finished and headed into the mediums' room for a cup of tea. It was during our conversation then that I asked how she was and she told me about a strange thing that had happened to her.

'Darling,' she said, 'I had a lovely experience in the back of a taxi while on my way to the Arthur Findlay College at Stansted two weeks ago.'

I wondered what she meant.

'Well, the taxi had just turned into the private road leading to the front of the college when I found myself out of my body.'

I enquired whether this had been an out-of-body experience.

'No,' she replied. 'I felt myself being taken over into the spirit world, where I could see my loved ones, and though I was aware of the taxi driver speaking to me, I was quite with the people on the other side.'

I noticed that as she told the story she was smiling brightly and there was absolutely no trace of fear or anxiety; so much so, that I also smiled.

'Yes, darling,' she beamed, 'I think that the spirit world was giving me a dummy run at passing, and it felt magnificent.'

This was a medium who not only believed in the afterlife, she lived as though the thought of death never touched her. She was someone who, when the time came, would not fuss or struggle, but just let go and enjoy the experience.

'It felt so exciting,' she told me, 'and quite pleasurable, I must say.'

Two weeks later I was on my way to work in a spiritual

centre in North Wales when I received a phone call from the woman who was running my course asking me if I'd heard what had happened to Mary Duffy. I told her I hadn't and she explained to me that Mrs Duffy had been found dead in the back of a taxi outside the front entrance to the Arthur Findlay College that morning. She must have died suddenly on the short journey from the airport, as the driver said she'd been very bright and healthy when he'd picked her up fifteen minutes earlier.

All I could do was smile. I knew in my heart of hearts that the wonderful Mrs Mary Duffy had gone home, and I knew that she would have gone through the same exciting experience she'd described to me two weeks earlier in Edinburgh.

'How wonderful,' was my exact thought. 'How wonderful to be taken home in a taxi after life's long journey!'

Mary's passing and how she accepted it after her first experience showed me that if we can accept that we are all going to shake off this mortal coil at some point, then we can just get on with enjoying life in the meantime. That was truly something that the very lovely Mrs Duffy had learned in her long life in service to the spirit world. She didn't just believe in an afterlife, she lived her own philosophy.

There are many sceptics and cynics out there who will say that belief in an afterlife is just a fantasy born of longing after we experience the death of a loved one, but it's not just the experiences people have with mediums that indicate life after death – the idea that there is an eternal soul, spirit or mind that functions beyond the body has been part of our consciousness since we first walked upright on this planet.

How many people, on nearing death, have experienced visitations from deceased loved ones? How many have had a near-death experience and felt their life-force expand and move upwards? There are so many books on these kinds of experiences, and I think that after hundreds of thousands, maybe even millions, of people have described such things, the idea merits more than being put down to fantasy.

CONCLUSION

What's It All About?

There is so much still to be learned about human consciousness and I honestly believe that many good mediums have
shown over the years that there are tremendous possibilities
of learning more about this life and the functions of our
mind and what it is capable of. Even if you are not a believer
in life after death, I think if you were to read some of the
masses of evidence collected on the work of mediums over
the years, for example Sir William Crookes's report on the
work of D. D. Home, you would be forced to consider that
we are far more than we appear to be.

In my own work I have presented evidence to many sceptics over the years, and a great number of them have become
believers. The same can be said of any medium who works
from the heart and whose intention is to truly help people.

In an effort to provide proof, I have allowed my mediumship to be tested by scientists and journalists and men of the
cloth, not to mention a few para-psychologists.

I remember being asked by Professor Chris French of
Goldsmiths, University of London, if I would take part in a
live test on the ITV television programme *This Morning*. I
liked Chris French and always thought him a fair-minded
man, so I agreed to take part. His claim was that as a medium,
I was very good at cold reading. I reminded him that as a
hairdresser, I was extremely good at cold reading, but even

so, observing how people sat or moved didn't allow me to come up with accurate names, dates and addresses, etc.

The test Chris set me was to read for two women whom he would choose and who would both be blindfolded. The idea behind this was they would not see the reader. Chris would also read for them and then they would decide who was the real medium/psychic and who was the impersonator.

I believe the good professor hoped that we would both be so general in our readings that the women would find it hard to distinguish who was who, therefore demonstrating that all readings were general and that mediums just used cold reading. Sadly for him, both subjects in the test said that the information they got from medium number one, which was me, was much more evidential – things like exact names, dates that were important to them and their loved ones, how their loved ones had passed on, etc. They also said that Chris, medium number two, was very general in his information and provided little or nothing of any importance.

Our little test was performed on the live television show and at the end the good professor concluded that the evidence showed I had done more than cold reading during the two sessions.

But at that moment, rather than feel vindicated, I realised that my task in this life wasn't to keep trying to prove my gift, but instead to use it where it was needed most. The people who watched that show wouldn't really have been converted to my way of thinking about the afterlife if they hadn't already been interested in it, and those who believed anyway wouldn't have been put off by Chris's tests, whatever the result.

Those who believe, believe; those who are adamant that there is nothing after death wouldn't be convinced if Albert

Best, Helen Hughes and Estelle Roberts were all to do their best work right in front of them.

So, what's it all about?

The True Message

I truly feel that our search for answers is quite personal and we will only find them through our own experiences. Some people do, of course, choose not to look. I believe that some go through this life almost asleep, that their conscious mind is numb because they do not wish to face the harsh reality of the physical and emotional world of which we are a part.

Personally, I find that when you see and hear spirits that no one around you can see or hear, and when you are taken to friends of your parents and they claim you are a medium and that you will travel the world and teach people about life after death, that should at least make you look at what life is trying to tell you.

I may be a rather extreme example, but the point is that my search led me to the life I have now, and that process is the same for all of us. I believe that the spirit world is giving us *all* the message that we should awaken to our true self, our spirit, and understand who and what we really are and why we are here. We should open our eyes to the reality of life. When we do so, the path we should be taking will open up before us.

It took me quite a while to get the true message that the higher mind of spirit was sending to me, and sending to others through me, and had been sending to everyone, through so many mediums, for so many years. That message was never about death, but about life.

The sensationalism that has surrounded some mediums has often distorted that message. When I look at the number of people, just in my own life, who have understood what I do as 'contacting the dead', I can understand how far away so many people are from the actual reality of mediumship. Mediums are never in contact with the dead – they are messengers for the *living*. They are passing messages from those who are living on in the spirit world and who want to convey this to their grieving loved ones in this world. That's what's really happening with mediumship.

The Call to Awaken

I know that grief can be so heavy that it can plunge people into a waking coma. They are stunned by their loss and dragged down by the emotional burden. That's why the evidence I have chosen to highlight in this book has sometimes been quite extreme. That has been needed to shock the recipient into awakening.

It is the very nature of spirit to want to wake us up and remind us that we are better and bigger than our human selves. In the early times before Spiritualism, this was done through phantoms and ghostly figures giving guidance and messages to help people, or through saintly people who, it would seem, had been chosen for that role. When we had evolved enough to stop burning and torturing people for their abilities to hear or see spirits and to investigate new discoveries and philosophies instead, the spirit world gave us new phenomena to examine in the form of physical mediumship.

Before and during the First World War, spirits appeared in darkened séance-rooms, shaping their former image out of ectoplasm and speaking through cone-shaped objects in direct voice mediumship, but only to small numbers of people who had chosen to gather for such occasions. During the Second World War, the spirit world worked through mental mediumship such as trance, clairvoyance and clairaudience, only now the mediums were speaking to crowds of hundreds and even thousands at a time.

The reputable mediums of old worked with sincerity to bring through evidence to show that life continues after physical death, and though many charlatans rose up to impersonate their talents for monetary gain, they somehow managed to convince many serious minds that their spirit messages were real.

I wholeheartedly admire many of those mediums, and the many great men and women who studied them and believed in the philosophy they presented and the phenomena they displayed. And I would say that what they did and how they did it were quite right for the time.

But times move on. I don't believe that a higher, more evolved mind – the higher mind of spirit – would stay static and appear the same to generation after generation, and so it has proved. It is only history that remains static; spirit is a living consciousness. So, inevitably, communication between the spirit world and the people of this world has changed. The darkened séance room has all but gone, and people want to see with their own eyes and feel with their own senses the phenomena of the spirit world on a higher, brighter level.

Mediums still try to help people who are broken after the loss of a loved one. In fact, there are hundreds of thousands of people today demonstrating spiritual practices. Some claim to bring messages from angels or ascended masters. There are thousands of people who call themselves channels and gurus and whose messages are not dissimilar to those of the mediums of the past. More and more people are turning to spiritual counsellors and life coaches. All in all, the spiritual supermarket of today can offer assistance in alternative practices from acupuncture to Zen.

What this tells me is that belief has changed and people are consulting an alternative practitioner the way they once would have consulted their priest, Rabbi or doctor. If I were to reveal the many highly respected people who have come to me over the years, I'm sure it would astound the general public, but to me they are just people who have had a loss, and no matter what their standing in society, it is natural for them to look for help and healing when their logic has run out of answers.

Over the years I have seen my own mediumship develop too. At first my gift worked through me in a similar way to the mediums of the Second World War. It attracted people to the idea of life after death and offered consolation to the grieving. It also led me to look up, as those earlier mediums did, and learn to raise my own spiritual vibration. Now I can see that my gift is being used more to bring people to the knowledge that you don't have to be a Spiritualist or a religious person of any kind to sit in the power of your own mind and develop a connection to your own higher spirit.

The way this connection is made has also evolved. In former times, people in development groups were taught to meditate by going within. The idea was that you were moving your mind into the deeper, darker parts of yourself to allow spirits to overshadow you and speak or create phenomena through you. But now, for some, that idea is claustrophobic. For me, and the people I sit in development with, meditation means going out of our physical body rather than within. We are moving into our light body, or subtler mind if you like.

This way of meditating makes more sense to me. The way I was first taught always felt a bit like hypnotism, in that we were taught to take our mind down to a deeper, heavier state. But the spiritual state is a much higher, brighter one than that of the dense human body, so for me the way to truly link with spirit is to lighten the mind and move out in an expanded, more vibrant way. It is to feel your own light energy, your light body, or spirit. It doesn't really matter what you call it, but if you can recognise your own spirit energy then you have a true way of recognising and interacting with other spirit energy.

It is in the recognition that we have a spirit body, a body that is vibrating at a different rate and existing on a different level, that enables us to understand that birth, life and death in the physical world are just changes in vibration. Understanding this fully, beyond thought or theory, means that there is inevitably a shift in the way we view this life and the life that will follow. I believe that the spirits who have guided me have led me to this understanding, to this point.

It may even be that what I call a spirit guide is really a higher, more advanced part of my own consciousness. I have often wondered about this. Could it be that the consciousness of humanity is evolving beyond the idea that the heavens are filled with angelic beings and spiritual masters? It may be that those ideas have been there because we have needed them, but our individual consciousness can develop to a stage where it can become spiritually self-supporting.

I believe that the forward movement of spiritual thinking will be to educate people in how to spiritualise themselves, something they can begin when they realise that there is more to them than a body and five senses. And when they accept that this life is not an accident and that there is a greater purpose behind it, which is to move beyond the fear-filled limited human existence into enlightenment.

Those who do wake up and acknowledge their spiritual nature find this awareness is often accompanied by a raw sensitivity which has to be understood and developed. I sense that many more people will develop, and will grow spiritually in a way that will one day be deemed normal. There will be no need for phenomena to convince people of spiritual reality, no need for support from an outer belief system, simply an inner desire to awaken and take spiritual responsibility.

I truly believe that as hard and difficult as this world seems at times, there is a genuine spiritual shift coming that will enable people to wake up *en masse* and realise that it is their responsibility to grow spiritually and move away from fearful, selfish, chaotic thinking – the type of thinking that has caused people to desire rather than share and to fear rather than love.

Any new way of living will happen in thought before it is realised in action. The physical world is an expression of the mind that governs it and that mind is on the verge of waking up. There have been many special times when there has been great change on this planet – great change in thought. A new dawn such as this is coming soon.

Living Life

In my life I have spoken to hundreds of thousands of people, if not millions, through my books and the documentaries I have featured in for various broadcasters. And on occasion I have been able to produce a level of mediumship that has convinced a wavering mind of life beyond what they believed was the end.

Like Mrs Mary Duffy, the lady who started me on this journey, I look forward to that new life with great excitement, because I know that my consciousness will not end but transform.

But before that, I will live. I will live this earthly life to the fullest, no matter what it throws at me. I remember one of the simplest messages from my spirit guide, Chi: 'Death will not end your living being, but fear and worry will stop it from progressing and absorbing the true essence of the experience of life. Be not afraid of the highs and lows of physical existence, for they are why you chose to be there. Be happy and be good to one another and love will reign and fear will dissolve as snow in the sun's warmth.'

True wisdom indeed.

Now I can see that our goal is to try to always be happy and, in doing so, to make others happy too. If we can do good and love others, and ourselves, in this life, then our consciousness will expand and our mind will open to incredible possibilities.

If what I have shared in this book is evidence enough for you that we are spirits who will return to the higher realms when our work here is done, then I ask you to take that evidence and move on, seeking other paths of enlightenment until you feel at one with life and death and the journey thereafter.

Our spirit is for ever. The spirit world will persist in bringing this message to us, through mediums and other means, until we learn that death is nothing to fear because it does not mean the end. Death is but a change; it is the doorway into for ever. This I know beyond reasonable doubt.

Further Reading

I have been practising mediumship for most of my life in one way or another, and I have studied the subject for most of my adult life and will continue to until it is my time to cast off the physical shell and step back into the spirit world. Even though I have had many amazing episodes and experiences on my spiritual journey, I am still looking for ways to help make the evidence, and maybe even proof, of our spiritual nature available for other searchers on the same path.

It is my advice to look deeply into the subject if you are interested, as scraping the surface won't reveal much to you. When my good friend Professor Archie Roy was accused of dabbling in the workings of mediums, he said. 'Oh, I don't intend to dabble in them, I intend to immerse myself in them.'

So, where to start? A lot has been written about mediums, particularly the mediums of previous generations, mainly because so many of them allowed themselves to be tested before they demonstrated their gifts. The Society for Psychical Research in London has masses of books and documents containing studies into mediums of the past. If you wish to delve into the past evidence of mediumship, this might be a good place to start.

There are also loads of books still available on physical and trance mediumship. Some of these highlight the fakes and charlatans, and these are worth reading also, because examining how the cheats worked helps in learning to understand how they differed from the mediums who were deemed to be credible.

Here are a few of the books that I personally have found most helpful:

Rosalind Cattanach, *Nan Mackenzie: Healer and Medium*, Garden City Press, 1982

—, *'Best' of Both Worlds: A Tribute to a Great Medium*, Pembridge Publishing, 1998

Reverend David Kennedy, *A Venture into Immortality*, Colin Smythe Ltd, 1973

Ernest Oaten, *That Reminds Me: A Medley of Personal Psychic Experiences*, Two Worlds Publishing Company, 1938

Estelle Roberts, *Forty Years a Medium: The Autobiography of Estelle Roberts*, 1959; updated as *Fifty Years a Medium*, 1969, reissued SDU Publications, 2006

Bernard Upton, *The Mediumship of Helen Hughes*, SDU Publications, 2006

The Robertson–Roy experiments:

Robertson, T J, Roy, A E. 'A preliminary study of the acceptance by non-recipients of medium's statement to recipients.' *Journal of the Society for Psychical Research* 2001; 65(2): 91–106.

Roy, A E, Robertson, T J. 'A double-blind procedure for assessing the relevance of a medium's statements to a recipient.' *Journal of the Society for Psychical Research* 2001; 65(3): 161–74.

Roy, A E, Robertson, T J. 'Results of the application of the Robertson–Roy protocol to a series of experiments with mediums and participants.' *Journal of the Society for Psychical Research* 2004; 68(1): 18–34.

Acknowledgements

Arthur Findlay. *Looking Back*, Psychic Press 1955
The Arthur Findlay books are the exclusive property
of The Spiritualists' National Union'

Ernest Oaten, *That Reminds Me: A Medley of Personal
Psychic Experiences*, Two Worlds Publishing Company, 1938
With kind permission from the Two Worlds Publishing Co

Bernard Upton *The Mediumship of Helen Hughes*
SDU Publications 2006
Estelle Roberts *Fifty Years A Medium*,
SDU Publications 2006
With kind permission from SDU Publication

Do you wish this wasn't the end?

Join us at www.hodder.co.uk, or follow us on
Twitter @hodderbooks to be a part of our community
of people who love the very best in books and reading.

Whether you want to discover more about a book
or an author, watch trailers and interviews, have the
chance to win early limited editions, or simply browse
our expert readers' selection of the very best books,
we think you'll find what you're looking for.

And if you don't,
that's the place to tell us what's missing.

We love what we do, and we'd love you to be part of it.

www.hodder.co.uk

@hodderbooks

HodderBooks

HodderBooks